Reckless Observations

Swerve

of a Postmodern Girl

Aisha Tyler

DUTTON

DUTTON
Published by Penguin Group (USA) Inc.
375 Hudson Street, New York, New York 10014, U.S.A.
Penguin Books Ltd, Registered Offices: 80 Strand,
London WC2R 0RL, England
Penguin Books Australia Ltd, 250 Camberwell Road,
Camberwell, Victoria 3124, Australia
Penguin Books Canada Ltd, 10 Alcorn Avenue,
Toronto, Ontario, Canada M4V 3B2
Penguin Books (NZ) Ltd, Cnr Rosedale and Airborne Roads,
Albany, Auckland 1310, New Zealand

Published by Dutton, a member of Penguin Group (USA) Inc.

First Printing, February 2004
10 9 8 7 6 5 4 3 2 1

Ⓓ REGISTERED TRADEMARK—MARCA REGISTRADA

LIBRARY OF CONGRESS CATALOGING-IN-PUBLICATION DATA
has been applied for

ISBN: 0-525-94806-6

Printed in the United States of America
Set in Palatino

This book is printed on acid-free paper. ∞

Contents

Introduction/Apologia

The ideas expressed herein are entirely those of the author (except for the ones she will disavow later when she comes to her senses).

You may be piqued, upset, scandalized, offended, or even enraged by some of what you read here. When this happens, please remember that the author is trying, first and foremost, to be funny. Which is quite difficult to do without offending *someone* at some point. Also remember that she's sorry, she doesn't know *what* the hell she was thinking.

At several points in the book, I may repeat or contradict myself. You'll get over it eventually. It's not a mathematical proof.

Any resemblance to actual people, either living or dead

should, in retrospect, have been obscured more efficiently by the author. Names have been changed to protect the innocent, the guilty, the hard of hearing, the perpetually drunk, the personally irresponsible, the morally corrupt, and the mentally unbalanced.

And to keep me from getting a beatdown.

Swerve

Sex, Drugs, and Postmodern Chicks

I wish I was more clever.

Everybody has that list, that internal list of wishes, those top five (or ten, or fifteen, whatever, I'm not counting) things you wish you were more of. Smarter, taller, a better cook, a faster reader, more patient, able to speak Spanish instead of just putting the vowels *o* and *e* on the end of English words and hoping people understand you,[1] a better singer, not such a chronic nose picker. Cleverness is number one on my wish list. I wish I was more clever.

Clever is not smart. Lots of smart people are not clever. Smart people can work out a math problem or expose and

---

1. As in, "please put el fan-o in el corner-o." This phrase was actually uttered in all sincerity by someone I know at a hotel in Mexico. The look she got from the hotel staff could have curdled flan. However, el fan-o, did in fact, end up in el corner-o.

dissect the flaws within the Hegelian dialectic (I don't really know what that means, but it sounds insanely thinky) or tell you who the president of Iceland is. All good things, yes, but not dazzling per se. Clever people, on the other hand, can figure out the safest way to get out of a car when it's teetering on the brink of a cliff, and how to fix a camera with a paper clip, and how to pitch a tent in the wilderness using just a pocketknife, downed branches, and beetle dung. They make music and write poetry and wear culottes with clogs and somehow still look stunning. Clever people are cool without trying.

Damn them.

When I had to name this book, I wanted a clever title, something that was funny and ironic and not too earnest. That is where the word *postmodern* comes in. In his book *Sex, Drugs, and Cocoa Puffs*, Chuck Klosterman offers two definitions of the word *postmodern*: a) "any art that is conscious of the fact that it is, in fact, art;" and b) "any art that is conscious of the fact that it is, in fact, product." These are both very cool, clever things, all thinky and arty and, well . . . postmodern. I had originally intended the word *postmodern* to mean someone who is not of the baby boom generation, or the me generation, or the x generation—not caught up in a political movement or a cultural sea change or a generational nadir—just trying to live their life, find personal and political fulfillment in whatever way is meaningful to them. All of this while having a really, really good time. Because honestly, why did all those other generations go through all that marching and demonstrating and Kombucha tea drinking if not so that we can get what we want and have a kick-ass time doing it?

So, what about the *Cocoa Puffs* definitions? Does this book really qualify as postmodern? Do I? Honestly, I have no idea. Apparently I didn't know what *postmodern* actually meant until I read Klosterman's book (and I am woman enough to admit that). I thought it meant *after* modern. (I can be a rather literal thinker—thus my desire to be more clever.) The Microsoft Word dictionary defined it as "relating to art, architecture, literature, or thinking developed after and usually in reaction to modernism, returning to more classical or traditional elements and techniques." Does that mean I should have typed it on an old Smith Corona typewriter? Or written the book longhand by the light of tallow candles? Or had it typeset by a letterpress printer? What classical elements and techniques are they talking about? And if I'm a postmodern girl, does my return to classical techniques mean I wear a corset under my Puma sweatsuit? Go back to wearing belted menstrual pads? Leave the house in plastic rollers and house shoes? This definition seemed weird, abstract, and more than a little irrelevant.

Klosterman's definitions made more sense and seemed more applicable to the book, but I still wasn't sure. So I went through and thought of all the things the book was trying to say, and what it wasn't, and if any of that could be construed as postmodern. I take "any art that is conscious

~ SWERVE ~

3

of the fact that it is, in fact, product" to mean any art that refuses to be earnest. Let's see if I hit the mark.

All the things this book is not (and a few things that it is)

This book is not a memoir or an autobiography. I don't for a second pretend to think that I have lived a long enough or interesting enough life to start memorializing it on paper. I mean *really*—I'm just a kid, and have been bobbling around on this planet for only a minute or so. While I'm sure I have done a few pretty ridiculous things, they're nothing I'm comfortable enough with at this point to share with you. Some of them happened only yesterday. I'm still smarting from the embarrassment. The rest of it, while fascinating to me, probably wouldn't even raise your eyebrow. I'm sure that at some point my life will make a very interesting, if scant, memoir. Probably not even a very scandalous one, although I did have a couple of emotionally wrenching days in the third grade that I'm sure will make for juicy reading.[2] I need another fifty years or so to scratch up some really exciting stuff before I can start prattling on about my big ol' important life. In the meantime, I'll keep it to myself.

This book is not about casual sex. Although if that's what *you're* after, more power to you. Many great women

2. You haven't suffered until you've had a group of kids tease you while dancing around you in a circle like you're a human maypole. That stuff leaves some nice, thick emotional scars. But that's for another book.

fought and died (well, they didn't die, but it does cut a more dramatic figure, doesn't it?) for the sexual revolution. They *burned their bras*, for chrissake and, if you want to skank it up, be my whorey guest. But fergawdsakes use a condom. I am not an advocate of casual sex, although I am an advocate of women getting what they want. This is something guys believe in with great fervor, even when they don't deserve it. Guys as a gender have one giant collective delusion of grandeur. No matter how lumpy and misshapen, no matter how few teeth or hair follicles, no matter what unholy smells emanate from their personage, they twirl the vision of themselves in bed with the Bud Light twins around in their heads like a giant mental jawbreaker, sucking feverishly on a fantasy that is never to be. It's a ridiculous way to live and, at the same time, quite poetically tragic. It has a strange beauty to it.

We, the more rational sex, will have none of it. We are practical, we are conservative, we *settle*. There's no sexy twin jawbreaker for us to suck on, oh no. We allow ourselves a nice healthy Fig Newton, or perhaps one of those awful oblong confections made of sesame seeds that your best friend's hippie mom always tried to convince you was real candy when you knew deep down it was a mind-control device. But you gnawed on it anyway, because far be it from you to say no to a generous offer, no matter how distasteful. And that is how we think, we girls. "This is the best I can do! Better make the best of it!" we chirp gaily. "I can handle the insensitivity, the paucity of regular phone calls, the emotional distance, the laziness in bed, the mysterious late nights, the even more mysterious cold sores. It's good for me! It'll make me strong! I'm going to love those cold sores *right off his face!*" That is *our* collective delusion, our great big oblong piece of sesame candy. Guys aspire, we concede. I, for one, think it's about high time for that to end. So while I don't think you should run out and jump every guy with a full set of teeth and a car that runs, if you did, I wouldn't judge you. I'm not about judgment. You do *you*.

Wait a minute. I'm thinking, and I guess this book *is* about sex, on some level. I mean, there *is* some stuff about sex in here. People like that sort of thing. People like sex. Sex sells. It seems to be doing quite a job for lite beer right now, not to mention rap videos. I understand it may even sell some books. So there is some sex stuff in here. (If you've already lost patience with this part of the book, go on, you perv, flip ahead. But if you're looking for diagrams or blurry amateur photography, you will be dismayed, my friend.) You got to give the people what they want, and since people tend to want money, power, and sex, there's some stuff about sex in here. Sorry, I don't have anything about how to get money and power. If I knew how to do that, a ghostwriter would be writing this right now, chained to my desk with a crust of moldy bread and a bowl of milk to sop it in, rather than me, pounding away here on my seventeenth cup of coffee, wishing to high heaven I had thought of an easier way to spend my summer.

This is not a self-help book, either. I don't have any steps, or exercises, or encounters, or affirmations, or recipes, or points, or any of that crap. If that stuff has worked for you in the past, rock on. I am incredibly lazy when it comes to things like journals and points, and invariably have lapsed out of every system, program, experience, or seminar I have ever taken part in. I have dozens of unfinished diaries, half-assembled models, instruments I haven't learned, languages I'm barely proficient in, trips I haven't taken. It's okay. I've made peace with the fact that I may never alphabetize my CDs, or turn that plastic crate of snapshots into a beautifully assembled silk-covered album. I'm actually starting to see my divine disarray, my consistent inconsistency, as a gift, as my own little quirky way of being. You always hear about great people having peculiarities, habits, and rituals that seem strange but are the key to their success. Lakers coach Phil Jackson's got Buddhism and strange facial hair. Martha Stewart sleeps four hours a night and eviscerates her underlings (thus proving my theory that she's a vampire). Tiger Woods has a lucky shirt (although, let's be frank, that guy doesn't need much luck). I am luckily lackadaisical. And I'm okay with that. You should be, too. Eek, I just sounded all self-helpy!

Ahem. As I was saying, this book is not a self-help book, mainly because I am not an expert on anything (except maybe pancakes and Saturday morning cartoons). I could say that I was an expert, make up some degree or life-changing experience that would give me the authority to tell you all the ways in which you are wrong, and I am right, about how you should live your life. I could compose a bunch of homey sayings like "If that man was a wheel, he wouldn't roll to the corner!" Or, "You can't get honey out of a beehive without going to the emergency room for anaphylactic shock." Or, like my daddy used to say, "Stop hogging the potatoes." But I won't, because I'm not an expert, I don't pretend to be one, and homey sayings make my head hurt. It's not that I don't think self-help books help people, or that they are all a bunch of hooey. It's just that I think *a lot* of them are hooey. Really high-priced hooey, with audio tapes and weekend retreats and frozen-food programs and murky homeopathic liquids and strange healing technicians who seem to have gotten their training from the back of a wheat-grass juice box. Keep this between us, but I have a sneaking suspicion that a lot of that stuff is designed to make you . . . *spend money*. It's just a theory of mine. That being said, thanks so much for spending money on this book. The accompanying frozen-food program and homeopathic weekend retreat will be coming to a civic center near you very soon. Just follow the scent of wheat-grass juice.

So. That's it. No affirmations, no diet tips, no tearful confessions, some stuff about sex, and quite a few curse words. If that's not refusing to be earnest, I don't know what is. I guess I could blow off writing the book, but then I'd have to give the advance back, and I don't think they'd take a used PlayStation 2, an empty beer ball, and a half-empty box of Krispy Kremes.

A confederacy of one dunce

Through the roughshod process of elimination I finally figured out what the hell I was trying to do. I was completely clear on what the philosophical thrust of the book would be. It made perfect sense in my head. The problem was, I couldn't explain it to anyone else.

At lunch with my publicist

Publicist: So, what's the book going to be about?

Me: Um, well . . . it's kind of a book about women . . . and guys . . . and sex.

Publicist gakks on her Cobb salad. (Note: gakking is a lot like choking, only louder and more life-threatening)

Publicist (turning purple): *What?*

Me: Calm down! It's not a how-to book!

On the phone with my manager

Me: More like a philosophical book about how I see the world, and women, and guys, and sex and stuff.

Manager (yawning): That sounds *fascinating*, but I don't know how you're going to have the time to devote to write a philosophy book. How long are those things, anyway, like a thousand pages?

At a bar with my middle-school best friend (male)

Me: It's just going to be like, a really funny book, with stories, and some advice, and kind of my whole perspective on dudes and dating and sex and stuff.

Best Friend (droplet of beer dangling pendulously from lip): So . . . is it going to be *dirty?*

On the phone with my mother

Mom: You always were such a good writer. I have no doubt it's going to be a great book. What's it about?

Me (long pause): Um . . . I can't describe it.

Mom: Well, you're screwed, honey.

I struggled like this for months.

Part of the problem was that I couldn't find any other book out there to compare it to, because as far as I knew, there wasn't any book out there like it (leave it to me to try to be goddamn *different* all the time). I wanted to do something different but, apparently, what I wanted to do was *so* different I couldn't articulate it to anyone else. I was getting worried and a little frustrated that I couldn't sum up *my own book* in a few words. I was also starting to sound slightly stupid in social situations.

At a party

Hollywood-suit-type guy: So, I understand you're writing a book.

Me: Yeah.

Long, juicily awkward silence.

Hollywood-suit-type guy: Yeah, so I'm going to hit the bar.

Me: Yeah, me too.

Okay, so not only did I have to write a book that I seemed incapable of describing to others in even remotely intelligible terms, but I was starting to doubt that I even had an idea for a book in the first place.

I was starting to think that it was a bad idea.

A couple of months into my writing period, I hadn't done more than jot down a few incoherent notes and avoid repeated calls from my editor. I was starting to dream up new and varied ways to fake my own death in order to get out of having to write this amorphous glob of a non-book. And then fortune, in the form of a cocktail-sodden party weekend, smiled upon me. Or more accurately, barked in my ear.

The Philosophical Origins of Swerve

or

Why and How to Be
a Badass

I'm in San Diego for the Super Bowl. Some friends of mine have flown into town to meet me, essentially to spend three days partying (we never do go to the game, preferring to watch it from the comfort of the lobby of the W Hotel, where there is catering and cocktails and a variety of fine products meant to nurse a hangover). The town is packed to the hilt with crazed Raiders fans, who are running through the streets in short-shorts and mesh half-shirts, baring lovely, taut, fur-lined beer guts and screaming "gobbledygook!" as loud as their booze-soaked lungs will allow. (It wasn't really the word *gobbledygook*, but Raiders fans are already unintelligible when they're sober. Fill 'em to the rim with the rich taste of malt liquor, and they start speaking Martian.)

So it's Saturday night, and we're all crammed into an SUV, on our way to a pre–Super Bowl party. The SUV is being piloted through aforesaid doomsday mayhem by a guy who's clearly just earned his driver's license, and who seems to be taking every wrong turn available. The longer we drive, the further we are from our destination. Tooth-less football fans scream as we creak by, waving glowsticks and pounding their chests like tiny King Kongs. Their idea of team spirit is to shriek "Number One, Baby!" into the darkened windows of cars, gnashing their bared teeth like loopy Maori youth. I start to imagine our car being rolled over and torched by a crowd of flesh-eating zombies chanting "Warriors! Come out and play-ay!" I'm dressed in some ridiculously tiny outfit (irony of ironies, there's going to be a red carpet at this thing), with stiletto heels which will hobble me terribly should I have to run for my life, but, I think, could be used as a weapon if I got cornered by a team of bloodthirsty killers with fangs and a pony keg. I start to sweat, which makes my hair slowly but surely puff out toward an inevitable Afro shape.[3] As I perspire and contemplate my horribly impractical Louboutins, my friend Nick leans forward from the backseat and asks, once again, the dreaded question:

3. The chemical nexus between black women's hair and environmental moisture has been well documented; I won't bother explaining it here, as that could take years.

Stuffed in aforementioned SUV

Nick: So what's up with this book?

Me (feeling nauseated): Well, um . . .

Nick (not waiting for an answer—he never waits for an answer): Eddie told me you're writing a book for girls about how to be a badass.

Me (long silence; lightbulb slowly materializing over my damp, frizzy head): A-hah! Yes! That's it!

This is a book for girls about how to be a badass.[4]

I was kind of pissed that a guy came up with it instead of me, but so be it. They're occasionally good for something.

So. How to be a badass. What does that mean?

It's not about learning how to start a bar fight or cut people with broken bottles or cauterize your wounds with pure grain alcohol. If I had to find an established idea to compare it to, I would compare it to the *mack*. If you don't recognize the word, it gained currency in the 1970s, popularized by the 1973 blaxploitation flick *The Mack*, starring Max Julien and Richard Pryor, which I, like many, have never seen. (I was in diapers. It would have been entirely

---

4. Boys can read it, too. Really. Don't worry, it won't bite. At least not until it gets to know you better.

inappropriate. Plus, I couldn't speak English yet.) I am, however, intimately familiar with it, because it is just *that* kind of movie. Like if *Shaft* is the *Halloween* of black films, then *The Mack* is *The Rocky Horror Picture Show*. You've never seen it, but if prodded, you could probably do the Time Warp again.

The concept of the *mack* is an old one. A *gigolo*, a *pimp*, a *player*—all words used over the years to refer to someone, a *male* someone, who plays by his own rules. All of these terms, in varying degrees, have come to have a positive connotation: a guy who gets the ladies, a lover, a manipulator of women and rubes. This connotation is so powerful and pervasive that Hugh Hefner can go out with eleven matching pneumatic blondes and be thought of as an international *bon vivant*, while Demi Moore appears in public with both her ex-husband and her twenty-five-year-old boyfriend and people faint dead away, their hands frozen in the shape of a cross. A woman who plays the field is the modern equivalent of a gorgon—one look and you are turned to stone.

Imagine a female version of James Bond, a woman who bedded tasty young things at whim, then discarded them for other, tastier, younger things with utter abandon. A woman who had sex with guys after knowing them for scarce seconds, guys with names like Ereck Chun, Dicky Galore, and Stiff E. Cockenstein (he would wear a monocle, I'm sure of it). She wouldn't be seen as debonair and worldly, she'd be seen as slutty and otherworldly. Madonna, in other words.

This dichotomy, this double standard, is such an old one it's growing a beard. In *The Scarlet Letter*, Hester Prynne is branded an adulterer when she sleeps with another guy after her husband has been missing for a year. An *entire year!* The guy's lost at sea, doesn't show up at the appointed meeting place, no messenger on horseback, no letter in a bottle, nothing. Back then, that pretty much equaled dead. And, let's make no bones about it, we'd have all done the same thing under those circumstances. Some of us wouldn't have waited *that* long: "He's been gone a fortnight! Clearly he's dead! I got the ale, you bring the mead! Let's get it on!" So understandably, lonely old Hester Prynne tries to get a little lovin', as she's entitled to do, and what happens? She's made to waltz about town with that big old A on her vestments (that's what they called them back then, *vestments*) looking to all the world like a colonial cheerleader. And what happens to the boyfriend? He goes down too, but not because he cheated. Oh no. Because he lied about it. If he had hopped up on the town stockade and hollered, "Yeah! I did it! I got me a little colonial poontang!" they probably would have hoisted him up on their shoulders and feted him all the way to the nearest barnraising.

If a man cheats on a woman, he has a mistress. There's

no word for what he's done to the wife, as if this is just an accepted hazard of married life. But if a woman cheats on a man, the man has been cuckolded. *Played. Dissed.* You can see where I'm going here. I'm not advocating infidelity, by any means. (Don't get ahead of me here, it's still early. Even I don't know what I'm going to say.) I'm just exploring why it is that no matter who does what to who, that polarization persists. The mack and the slut. We can't seem to escape it.

You'll notice that there are no corresponding terms for the woman who gets what she wants. The corresponding term for a female *bonne vivante* lives somewhere in *slut* and *ho* territory. I find that so tiresome I can't even put it into words. It is an archaic, sexist double standard that is so unbelievably played out that it almost wouldn't even merit discussion if it weren't still so unbelievably prevalent. This is something you learn from a young age, usually sometime in middle school (earlier nowadays—oof!): guys who get around are cool, girls who get around are sluts.

Now I'm not advocating "getting around" for *anyone.* Really, I'm not. I toss that burden to Heidi Fleiss. (Or I would, if her brittle bones could sustain more than her own quavering eighty-six pounds.) I'm just questioning why, in this day and age, it's okay for guys and not for girls. Where are these guys getting all this sex from, anyway? Hmmm? If all the girls are required to be good, and the boys required to be bad, all guys must be having sex with the same three or four town harlots over and over again.[5] Not much to brag about, hm?

The old *player* versus *slut* paradigm persists. It refuses to die. Why is that? Part of the reason is that we perpetuate it ourselves. Yes, *we*. We girls. We call other girls slutty, look them up and down, roll our eyes, suck our teeth, and generally do our best impression of Jackée Harry after a couple of stiff Margaritas. We don't admire girls who get what they want—we envy them, or pity them, or, worse yet, we fear them. And as my good friend Yoda once said, "Fear leads to anger; anger leads to hate; hate leads to suffering; suffering is the way of the dark side." Or *something* like that. That Yoda. For a short guy, he's pithy.

So what to do? What to do? We need to find a way to exalt the girl who gets it all, the girl who goes for what she wants without fear of recrimination or reprobation, the girl who is in control, making her own money, driving her own car, drinking red wine with seafood, charging headlong toward her destiny.[6] For the sake of discussion, let's call this girl *"the mackette."*

Now please realize I am not talking about the girls you see in rap videos "dropping it down" and "backing it up" and "doing that right thurr" while it's "hot in herre." In addition to them being way too free with their "rr"s,

5. Aargh! See? I did it myself. It's insidious!
6. At this point, you should start to hear Destiny's Child crooning "Independent Women Part II."

these women aren't doing their own thing. They're doing someone else's thing. And badly. With too much makeup. And far too many visible panty lines. These women aren't in control. They are decoration, appetizers, set decoration for someone else's fantasy, content to pout and snarl and slither in whatever direction has the best camera angle. They may think they're being sexy, but the fact of the matter is, they're just being used. And if there's one thing a mackette does not do, it's let herself be used.

The sad thing is that these videoland women actually have real-life counterparts. You know these girls, the ones who show up at bars and clubs with all their physical assets on a platter, spilling over the top and out of the bottom and even sometimes out of the sides, hoping they can get whomever and whatever to pay them enough attention to raise their brittle self-esteem for a few paltry hours. These girls are not macking—they are begging. Begging for love, begging for attention, begging to feel powerful, begging to feel in control. But they aren't. How can they be? They've already put themselves in the unenviable position of advertising what they're about before they even open their mouths. There is a difference between being sexy because you feel sexy and being sexy because "Oh god please I need a guy to notice me so badly I'm erupting in a torrential flop sweat." See how the second one isn't so great?

Sexiness is not the way you dress. It's a state of mind. The state of mind the mackette lives in all the time—(cue

Barry White-esque baritone) *twenty-four-seven-three-sixty-five, baby.* And that is one badass place to be.

So I'm a one-woman advocate for social change. I believe that we cannot be free until we have shed this old, lame paradigm about women being chaste and men being wanton. The idea is not that we all become wanton, without regard for our own physical and emotional health, indulging in urge and impulse with reckless abandon. The idea is that we should be entitled, as human beings, to be happy. We are entitled to be *satisfied*, whatever that word means to you. You are entitled to be and have what you want. You are entitled, to coin a very dogeared phrase, to be all you can be.

You are entitled to be a badass.

Why Society Hates You and Wants You to Fail

Okay, so that's a little dramatic. Society doesn't hate you. Society isn't even really a *thing*, is it? Maybe a better term is *pop culture*. That's it. Pop culture hates you and wants you to fail.

Pop culture is a sonofabitch.

Now I know I sound like some kind of low-rent Naomi Wolf, like one of those old-school feminists (There! I said the f-word! Get over it, cause there's more where that came from!) in a dirndl skirt and plastic clogs, kicking up a cloud of patchouli oil and pot smoke as I merrily burn a stack of fashion magazines. You may even be raising an eyebrow now, dear reader, and thinking, "Wait a minute . . ."

Inside my head (or yours, depending on which is more roomy)

Reader: Pop culture is bad? But you're, like, completely immersed in that world!

Me: Yes, yes, but this isn't about me. You're getting off the subject.

Reader: It *is* kind of all about you, isn't it? It's *your* book.

Me: Well, yes, it is, but right now we're talking about the world out there, about society, pop culture, the peer pressure of the masses.

Reader: Which you're saying is bad.

Me: Well, yes and no. Pop culture is great. But it *can* be bad, at times.

Reader: How?

Me: You know, the unattainable images of beauty, the hypersexualization of our youth, the pressure to be perfect, to be young . . .

Reader: Didn't I see you in the *Maxim* Hot 100? In your *underpants?*

Me (beat, sullen): They weren't *my* underpants.

Reader: That's kind of beside the point, isn't it?

Me: No it isn't . . . Hey! Whose book *is* this?

Back to business. My point is that there are a zillion jillion images and ideas and messages being fired at you at a million miles an hour all day every day, just like the giant television transmitter in Willy Wonka's chocolate factory. It's a constant barrage meant to get you to feel certain ways, some goodly, mostly badly, all of it intended to get you to buy stuff. *To buy stuff.* Now I'm not a communist. I believe in buying stuff. Hell, stuff's great. Some of my favorite stuff is stuff. I like clothes and shoes and makeup and music and movies and high-shine nail lacquer and thong underwear and convertible bras and tiny handbags shaped like puppies and energy drinks and clever hats and tampons with pearlized applicators and all of it. All of it. I do. But most of what sells it is stuff that makes you feel bad about how your life is now, and makes you think that if you could only have shiny nails and whiter teeth and a smoother bikini line and an easier time with your period, that you'd be happier and you'd fall in love and have a zillion babies and a giant urban assault SUV in which to transport them, zooming along with your ultrashiny gorgeous nails and your ultrashiny gorgeous hair and your ultrashiny gorgeous man who reeks of Davidoff Cool Water (or Axe Body Spray—it's usually on sale). Most of what we see and read presents it as that easy. If only!

Let's add to that this cultural obsession with matchmaking. There is an epidemic of reality shows that are hellbent on ruining whatever shred of self-respect and dignity we have when it comes to relating to the opposite sex. Rather than meeting and falling in love with other people in a natural, organic way, these shows make the whole courtship process seem as easy as taking a number at your neighborhood bakery, then desperately and frantically gnawing on each and every loaf of bread on the shelf until you find one that doesn't make you want to hurl.

Now I have a confession to make. I read *Us Weekly*. I love it. My relationship with *Us Weekly* is peculiar, furtive. It's a love-hate relationship, one that swings between elation and deep, jabbing shame.

Here's how it goes. I refuse to subscribe to *Us Weekly*. I refuse in a grand way, a dramatic, sweeping gesture way, in a *principled* way, to support *those* people. I will not send in my hard-earned twelve dollars to fund their rickshaw operation. I refuse because, at its core, *Us Weekly* is a tabloid. It preys upon the morsels and tidbits and detritus of celebrity lives, stealing images and appropriating what should be very private moments. Half of the photos in the magazine are clearly taken with a telephoto lens: shots of actors pushing their kids on swings or driving to the doctor's office or getting a falafel at the neighborhood deli. These photos are then arranged to look as if they were authorized, or at the very least *okay*, and not stolen. They are gilded and placed and couched in a way that makes you feel like, "Hey, really, this isn't invasive! They're showing us how celebrities are just like regular people! I go to the doctor's office! I *love* falafel! I'm not spying when I read this, I'm *relating*. I'm *empathizing*." It feels informal, almost newsy. You feel as if you are actually learning something about these people, something valuable, something relevant, when, in reality, you are fascinated by photos of them doing things that you do every day, without fanfare, usually unshowered and in clothes that make you look as if you ran away from a sanitarium. And no one takes your picture, because it's just not that important. So how is it that you shamble through your day, eating falafel and getting your birth control pills, feeling utterly mundane and everyday, and then run home to salivate over pictures of someone else doing the exact same thing? What is *that* about?

Us Weekly also adopts this bizarre kind of informality with its subjects, an intimacy that doesn't really exist. They'll take a shot of a celebrity, and then give it a little thought balloon, or a cute handwritten caption, or a banner written in the first person and chock-full of exclamation points, like "Our first date!" or "Me drunk and butt naked on a Mexican beach!" All are meant to imply that the fine people at *Us* actually know what the celeb was thinking at that time, perhaps took the photo with their permission like a friendly passerby would have done for a couple on holiday, may have even spoken to them directly about their thoughts and feelings as they were buying falafel or picking up their dry cleaning, when the truth is a dumpy guy in a trench coat and crumpled fedora took the photo from four hundred feet away, schvitzing all over his telephoto lens.

The problem for me is not the big moral statement I make by not subscribing. The problem arises for me in line at the supermarket.

The problem is, you see, that I cannot seem to resist this magazine's dirty, dirty siren call when I'm checking out at the store. I don't know if I'm especially weak when I'm shopping for groceries, if the hundred different choices and judgment calls and evaluations I have to make as I'm going through the supermarket: *Will I really eat these collard greens or should I just save time and throw them in the trash right now? If yogurt is blue, is it still yogurt? The fact that these cookies are shaped like kangaroos doesn't make them healthier. If I eat an entire pint of soy ice cream, is that as bad as eating an entire pint of real ice cream?* is so exhausting that by the time I get to the checkout I'm overwhelmed, weakened, my resolve worn down at precisely the time that that glossy, sparkly rag is calling out to me, promising to let me know just how hot (insert big pop star and A-list actress names here) romance really is. I try, really I do. I ball up my fists, grit my teeth, squint, look away. I try to find something interesting elsewhere. What about "Great Summer Salads" in *Bon Appetit*, or "Simplifying Your Closets" from *Real Simple*? Trash, all of it. Empty. Uninteresting. I want to know who was grinding on the dance floor of a popular Hollywood dance club. I want to know who threw up in the bathroom of a posh New York restaurant. I am very, very weak.

So I buy it, after all of my self-righteous refusals to subscribe. I buy it almost too often to mention, giving the lovely people at *Us Weekly* four times what they would make off me if I just gave in and sent off my twelve dollars.

I buy it, and I read it, cover to cover, sometimes before I've even pulled out of the parking lot. It's an awful, sparkling, glorious, terrible train wreck, and I can't look away.

Except for the features on reality dating shows. I won't read those. A girl has standards. I swish past them crisply, nose in the air, thinking superioristic thoughts, my pinkies raised so as not to be sullied by those subpar pages. I do not, I will not, support the crap trafficking of the dating shows. There is something so crass, so vacant and cold-hearted, so unbelievably unromantic, so *uncool*, about those shows that even brief consideration makes me feel unclean. They are throwbacks, arcane relics of a time when marriages were arranged and wives were bought and sold. It doesn't matter that they've got bachelorettes now, "choosing" the guy of their dreams. It feels like an afterthought, like a compensation, like a "See? We've got chicks now, so it's not sexist. It's equal opportunity creepiness!"

Conservative wonks and fundamentalist mouthpieces bark on and on about gay unions threatening the sanctity of marriage, having, apparently, never stopped to consider that every day, somewhere on the tube, there is a show in which people are coldheartedly engaging in the courtship of another, ostensibly with the goal of "holy" matrimony, jostling and neighing like colts on a track, sprinting after a carrot which is made of . . . money. And sometimes fame. That's it: a money carrot with a chewy fame center. These people don't care about marriage, or its sanctity, or even the romantic notions of matrimony, the happily ever after and the swooning delirium of betrothal. No. They want money, and infamy, and maybe a job on a television newsmagazine.

The essence of the premise remains the same—romance is a confluence of technical factors. Love can be authored, fabricated, constructed, especially when money and notoriety are involved. The reason we aren't all madly in love with the man or woman of our dreams is that we haven't allowed America to select our perfect mate from a cross-section of eligible singles using a combination of Internet and phone-in voting. The whole thing is so manufactured and skeevy that it could just as well be set in a Nevada brothel as on a television network. *Promenade; turn; you, no you; turn around; how are your teeth; bad kisser; back in line. Now, you, step forward; you seem nice; no, wait, you made an inappropriate joke; you're out of here. All right, number three, you seem like a nice guy; I'm starting to fall; oh, no, you have a police record that wasn't revealed in the pre-show vetting process, you will never do.* And so on. I think the technical term for all of this is *ick*.

Anyway, for some reason, one day, I decided I wasn't getting my money's worth out of *Us Weekly*. I scowled to myself, "I pay for this thing, and then I skip over the reality dating show section. That's four whole pages I'm missing out on. What a waste. I'm going to go back and read them and see what it is I'm missing, why people bother watching these shows at all." I righteously folded the pages back

28

and took a gander. Here was the headline: WILL THEY FIND LOVE? The article went on to present some frothy little tidbits about two female dating show "protagonists," giving their opinions on the guys they're "dating" on the show. It was all pretty forgettable, but I was particularly taken by a comment that Lisa Shannon, from the show *Cupid*, made about one of the dates. Her exact quote was "I like the blond hair; I've never dated a blond—it's fun."

What does that *mean?* How is it fun? What is it about a blond guy that makes dating him more fun than dating a brunet guy? When she goes out, does she ruffle up his blond hair with her hands until he looks like a clown, then laugh hysterically? Does his blond hair get them bigger portions in restaurants, or a better seat in movie theaters? Does his blond hair do tricks? Does he make balloon animals with it? What kind of a comment is that? My head was swirling. Mind you, this is a show in which Lisa will *marry* the guy America picks for her. She has to marry him, and *stay* married to him, for a year. If she does, they split a million dollars. Their incentive for fidelity is money, and money only. There is not one aspect of the entire experience that's authentic, even their declaration of love at series' end, because they *have* to say they love each other. For the *money*. It's all about the money.

Some would say that's the most postmodern experience of all—dating as art. Stripping the dating experience down to its purest elements: lying, manipulation, superficiality, greed, and false declarations of love. Because, really, isn't that most of what goes on in the dating scene? We all lie, cheat, and steal until we find the one person who cracks our façade, breaks through our defenses, makes us set down our arsenal of weapons, and come as we really are. Only we don't do it on television.

Shows like *The Bachelor*, *Who Wants to Marry a Millionaire?*, *For Love or Money*, and the latest affront, *Married By America*, present a cultural idea of courtship akin to caste-based, Indian-arranged marriage. A gaggle of what seem to be quite attractive, capable women (or men) struggle desperately to make one nugget-headed dim bulb with bleary-eyed acting aspirations fall in love with them. They scratch and fight and spit and generally embarrass our entire gender, most often with the added incentive of a million-dollar bounty at the end of the abject humiliation rainbow. So, we all watch that and think:

a. it's okay to be a desperate, venom-drooling gold digger;

b. if this is the best these gorgeous, able, employed women can do, then there is no hope in the world of anyone ever finding love, *ever*; and

c. authentic relationships, commitment, and marriage are a joke.

Of course, you're thinking, "Well, I'm not like those women." And of course you're not. Those women are desperate. For relationships, for attention, for validation, for a guy, *any* guy, even a guy who is mandated by contract to appear with them whenever they're in public, regardless of whether they'd like to press their thumbs into his eye sockets until they hear a satisfying pop. But an atmosphere of desperation fosters desperation. Dogs smell fear, and so can humans. We've got a cultural widespread panic, fueled by these orgies of schadenfreude, and the whole thing has the effect of putting us at a disadvantage, of making us feel less than, hunted, off-kilter and well . . . desperate.

The prevailing cultural attitude toward dating is that you can't get someone to love you without either strutting your stuff like a crack-addicted streetwalker or viciously stabbing other people in the back (or the face), and that women are just these *things* to be lined up and reviewed, chosen, or discarded, with a dismissive wave of the hand or a faux-sincere soliloquette of regret or, mayhap, a toss of a single long-stemmed rose.[7] All of these shows are filmy with a sticky, overwhelming haze of desperation.

7. Which, by the way, I believe there should be some kind of legislation against. The single long-stemmed rose has got to be the most hackneyed, insincere, predigested gesture in the entire arsenal of romantic gestures. It is the thing the guy goes to when he can't think of anything better. It doesn't require any imagination, or knowledge, or understanding of the individual woman it's being presented to. It has about as much thought and consideration behind it as the choice of whether to get fries with a cheeseburger. As such, it is the go-to choice for cheaters, liars, and all guys trying desperately to get laid. And, on top of it all, it's cheap. A guy who hands you a single rose, unless he's picked it out of a neighbor's yard or purchased it right in front of you from an old lady with a basket and a headscarf, should immediately be suspect. I'm just saying keep an eye on him.

So why do we watch? The people are creepy, the situations uncomfortable, all the kissing and sleazy proclamations of affection gross. Why do Americans keep tuning in? And don't tell me it's because we're romantics. These shows are about as romantic as bone-marrow extraction. There is nothing truly romantic about any of it. What holds the most attraction for us, the viewing public, *is* the schadenfreude.

Dating is hard. It's painful and upsetting and gut-wrenching and mortifying. We embarrass ourselves and others, we say the wrong thing, do the wrong thing, spit food while we're talking, tell inappropriate stories, pass gas (loudly) in nice restaurants. We act needy and whiny and depressed, call in the middle of the night, feel desperate for sex, have sex out of desperation. We are melting in a pool of regret and confusion, and the last thing we want to tune into is someone who's getting it right. On the contrary, what we enjoy seeing is someone who, with all of the funds and assistance and organization in the world, with a professional makeup artist and complementary lighting and a stylist, still can't seem to get it quite right. *Hah! Look at her! That was the most uncomfortable moment in the world! Finger-nails on a chalkboard would have been less agonizing! Oh, man did he say the wrong thing! If this was a cartoon his head would have turned into a donkey! What an ass! Whoo! She's crying! Weeping openly in front of everyone! Rejected on national televi-sion, that's gotta hurt! Man, I am glad I'm not them!*

We watch because we all want to know that no matter who you are, how beautiful or famous or chosen by God (or at least a team of network talent scouts) it can all still go horribly awry. The real satisfaction comes after the show is over, when the contestants' true feelings come out. Every relationship started on those early dating shows has failed. They were tenuous to begin with, forged in the heady glare of just-add-water fame and, as soon as the lights went off, you had two people staring at each other, each thinking the same thing. *I have spent a cumulative forty-seven minutes with this person. I'm not in love with them. I don't know them at all. What's more, they seem to be a bit of a fame-obsessed spotlight whore.* Since those (in)famous breakups, the shows have had to build in clauses and incentives to keep these couples together, to maintain the lie that they actually produce real relationships with real feelings that can exist outside of the vacuum of the seven-to-thirteen-week summer run. Two of those couples are still together.[8] Give it a few months.

Money or fame—there is no panacea, no insurance, for a successful relationship, and anyone that would consent to let ratings and Internet voters drive their personal lives deserves the ultimate and very dramatic letdown they get. Joe Millionaire's premise is to lure women, with the

---

8. Trista and Ryan from *The Bachelorette*, and Andrew and Jen from *The Bachelor 3*.

promise of money, to meet and fall for a guy they've never met. The rewards for the women are all consumable (pearls, rubies, emeralds), and they fight over dresses while the guy spends his time trying to divine which women are motivated by money and which aren't. It's a futile exercise. They *all* are. And so is he. That's the premise. And the rub.

So, what are these people thinking? The ones who sign up to be the bachelor, or the bachelorette, or the millionaire, or the cupidette, or whatever it is? The success rate of the couples from these shows is even lower than the success rate for regular Hollywood couples. Not only that, but every aspect of your personality, every flaw, every caprice, every bit of self-involvement and promotion, is splayed across the airwaves, then dissected on the Internet in threads longer than a deep-sea driftnet. We could chalk it up to that fifteen minutes of fame, that sense of entitlement we all have as Americans—that it is our birthright to be famous—but, as Evan Marriott has proven most handily, being a reality show protagonist gets you absolutely nowhere. Mariah Carey videos notwithstanding.

We know no one is legitimately falling in love on these shows, or expecting to find their soul mates. It's a lark. An exercise. A fun way to spend a couple of months, and afterward you get into some great Hollywood parties and get to talk to Pat O'Brien. Maybe go to the Playboy Mansion. That in and of itself is a jackpot for most of us. So they think, "What the hell, it's only television. If it doesn't work out, we'll get a divorce." Which is the exact same attitude that most of us have toward marriage and relationships. Which is why none of us really believe in true love, or commitment, or any of that treacle. Which is why we love to watch these shows, because it reinforces the low-level despair we've been nursing about ever finding true love. Which is why, when your congressman tries to get you to sign a petition saying that gay unions should be banned because they threaten the sanctity of marriage, you should send him over to Trista Rehn's house.

Hey, victory starts at home.

SWERVE

The *Sociopolitical Implications of Personal Grooming*

or

The Bikini Wax as Postmodern
Political Statement

FADE IN.

Neighborhood recreation center basement, Wednesday night. Folding chairs sit in a circle, as various men and women gather, sipping watery coffee from thimble-sized Styrofoam cups. I stand, head hung, and clear my throat.

Hi. My name is Aisha, and I am a professional grooming addict.

Hi Aisha!

My addiction to salon services is deep and wide-ranging. I've done it all, deep-tissue massage, the salt glow, the seaweed wrap, the Vichy shower. I've wasted whole days at the spa, half naked, guzzling herbal tea and stumbling from the steam room to the relaxation tank in a chamomile daze. I've paid for services I didn't need, binged on waxes and rubdowns, gotten two or even three massages, *one right after the other*. I know no shame.

We hear you, sister. We've been there. One day at a time, one day at a time.

But my drug of choice is the professional pedicure. The feelings I have for the salon pedicure are of a nature that should be reserved only for people. I think about it, daydream about it, miss it when I haven't had one in a while. The rush I feel as I slip my naked feet into that bubbling hot water, feel the massage jets tickle my arches like a tentative lover, inhale the heady scent of cuticle cream and nail polish remover, and hear the manicurist demand that I *pick a color!* is akin only to the golden, breathless moments before a very good orgasm.

Several people exhale, shift in their seats uncomfortably. One woman, visibly shaking, leaps up and runs from the room. I continue.

The worst part of it is . . . I've become an enabler.

There are gasps, clucks of dismay. I inhale, and go on.

I am driven by a force I do not understand—my love of the pedicure has made me an unwilling evangelist. I eyeball my friends' clawlike toes in disdain, sniff with disapprobation as they clip-clop around, their feet resembling ungulate hooves. I entreat other women to get foot services, beg, wheedle, even make spa dates to ensure they get the work done. I've been known to buy spa gift certificates for my girlfriends, and even a few guys.

I cast a look around at the cluster of my disapproving peers. I can't help it. It feels so good. I do not like to get pedicures. I *need* to get pedicures. It is as much a part of my life as showers and tooth brushing and Oreo binges. It is interwoven with the very fabric of my life, the connective tissues of my being, and if you are not getting them, sister, you are not living.

Mayhem. People leap to their feet, spilling coffee and overturning chairs. There is yelling and finger pointing, some tears. I am hit in the head with a Styrofoam cup. At this point, I am too far gone to care.

FADE OUT.

I wasn't always such a slave to hot-water grooming rituals. When I was younger, I had a very late-twentieth-century attitude about personal grooming. Which makes sense, because it was the late twentieth century. And because I was young, and therefore dumb. I lived "off the grid," as it were, when it came to the personal care industry. As far as I was concerned, all the plucking and waxing and coloring and creaming and polishing and rubbing and reaming and scoring was best left to Trump divorcées and porn stars—being a modern, sensible, self-confident, intellectual, self-actualized woman, making what could loosely be construed as a living as an artist, I didn't need to do these things. My beauty was inner, transcendent, glowing, ethereal, affecting, in need of no extraneous paring or gilding of any kind. I also felt that the industry that provides these products and services foments such feelings of overwhelming, eviscerating inadequacy among women as to be morally reprehensible and, therefore, valueless.

The old me

(shaking some candy-colored fashion rag in the air): These images of beauty are unattainable! No one could possibly have skin this smooth or an ass this tiny! When in the hell am I going to find the time to make a body-glow rub from kosher salt and French lavender? I don't even know what French lavender is! What makes it different from English lavender? And how the hell am I going to find some that's pesticide free?! I can't even find the time to keep a steady supply of clean underwear in my dresser! In fact, I'm wearing a pair of inside-out men's boxer briefs as I speak! This is outrageous! It's unrealistic, demeaning, soul crushing! I refuse to be this rube, this naïf, this pawn of the great industrial–beauty complex! I am taking a stand, right now! I am saying no to the marketing, no to the cajoling, the manipulation, the insistence that my lips be glossy, my toes buttery, and my skin hair free! I revolt!

I toss the magazine down triumphantly, my face beatific, my *eyes shining. Supermarket security surround me, wrestle me to the ground, handcuff me and drag me out of the store, but not before extracting $3.99 from my purse to pay for aforementioned, and now effectively destroyed, candy-colored fashion rag.*

The new me

A nice bikini wax never hurt anyone.

My love affair with professional grooming services started all at once. It was a grand, dramatic romance, and I was instantly hooked. It started innocently enough, with one, tiny service. Now I'm in so deep you could call me the spa's bitch.

I was going to Hawaii. It was my first time, and I had this idea that I was going to be fabulous. Every picture I've ever seen of a woman on the beach on a tropical island, she looks fabulous. Running down the beach, luxuriating under a waterfall, or reclining casually in a hammock, hibiscus in her hair (jaunty!), legs crossed daintily, bathing suit hiked up so high you imagine her digestive process has been temporarily interfered with . . . They always look fabulous. Nowhere have I ever seen a woman with visible body hair marching up her serpentine legs like a tiny ant army, or tufting delicately out of the edges of her bikini bottoms like she's been hiding a gremlin in her shorts and someone just doused her with water. These women are always perfectly hairless, like tall, tanned, besuited aliens. I did not feel so hairless. I needed some assistance.

Let me say first of all that I had given up shaving. Throughout high school and college I had occasionally shaved my legs, you know, for special occasions like junior prom, or senior prom, or the boat dance (because other than those times, who's going to see your legs anyway?) but I had always, and I mean *always*, cut myself. I am one of the klutziest people in the world. I think it has something to do with being tall, I dunno, but I am a walking self-inflicted injury. I could bruise myself with a marshmallow. So I had recently renounced shaving, because every time I tried it started fine, but ended with me holding a long strip of my shin skin in my hand like I had just trick-peeled an orange, crying uncontrollably.

Let me also say that once, and only once, I had tried to shave my bikini area. As if the fearsome proximity with which a razor blade passed my most precious bits and pieces wasn't enough, there is nothing like having a nick . . . down there. I'd rather have a toothpick in my eye. Add that to the unbearable itching which accompanies the stubble— that's right, I said *stubble*—and you've got yourself a party that lasts a day and a hangover that lasts three weeks. All in your pants.

A friend of mine said she met a stripper that shaved every day. *Every day.* I find that hard to believe. That is an extremely sensitive area (like I have to tell you that). That's like running a razor over your tongue every morning. Eventually you'd just form some kind of awful, inappropriately located callus. And there's nothing not-hotter than watching a half-naked sexual fantasy grasp the brass pole with one hand and scratch her naughty spot with the other. I doubt she gets many tips.

Anyway, after my extremely traumatic experience with the shaving and the slicing away of the flesh in strips and the incessant, uncontrollable scratching, I decided the only way I was going to be fabulous in Hawaii was to get professional help. Having never had a bikini wax, and having *very* little idea of what it was (other than a hair removal system, and that Joey Tribbiani once ate it during Ross and Rachel's breakup), I jumped in wholeheartedly.

I had no idea what I was in for.

The thing you need to remember, as someone is applying *hot* wax to your most delicate of nether regions—a special place touched only by yourself, your gynecologist, and a few (hopefully) very well-vetted suitors with impeccable hygiene—pressing strips of muslin cloth (why not silk? *why?*) against that wax, then ripping it away mercilessly, taking all of the hair and most of the top layer of skin with it, is that *you paid for this*. It was *your* idea to strip from the waist down, climb up on a paper-covered table, and let a girl, who clearly has no medical training, and with whom you have not made out beforehand, touch you, repeatedly, and in a most painful way, all about the pelvis. This process takes maybe ten minutes all told; of course, it feels like an eternity, like you are once again passing through the birth canal, like you are being pulled apart in sheets like a Hungry Jack buttermilk biscuit, like enduring the last twenty minutes of *Contact*. Oh ho, my friend, but you are not done. She then pulls out a set of tweezers. *Tweezers*. And she gets down there, and I mean *down there*, and starts *tweezing out the hair she missed*. Sometimes she has to pull on a particular hair repeatedly. Over and over. Until she tweezes it out. Sometimes this hair is very close to the place where all life originates. This does not seem to bother her. Neither do your screams of agony. She has a job to do, and she will do it. When you leave, your undercarriage will be like butter, like a bowling ball, like *whoa*. That is her mission. That is what you paid her to do. It matters none to her that this is the most intimate of places, that her face is inches from it, nay, centimeters, that her breath is ruffling your shorties, and that you are making nervous, completely inconsequential small talk in the hopes of diverting both of your attentions from the aforementioned gently waving shorties. This is a job to her. Even though this was a half day's instruction in beauty school (now called *aesthetician's college*—weighty), receiving less time in the curriculum than acrylic nails, even though you and she are the same age and from the right angle this could easily be a soft-core porn flick rather than a perfectly respectable beauty procedure, this is a job to her. She's seen one, she's seen 'em all and, by god, she's gonna send yours out shining like the morning sun.

The first time you have this done, you leave confused.

And limping. You wonder why you did it. You feel violated, slightly ashamed. You wonder if the other girls went through the same thing, or whether you got a special treatment, a little extra agony, on the house, because you had "that look in your eye." You gently rub your tenderoni with cream, or aloe vera gel, or a stick of margarine, and you vow, with god as your witness, never to do that again. You feel then much as you did the first time you had a horrible hangover. You hug yourself and rock back and forth and wail to the heavens, "Just get me through this, and I promise I will never, ever, do that again!" You sit gingerly. You feel rueful. You reward yourself with ice cream.

And then, in a couple of days, the pain subsides, and the angry redness fades, and you can once again cross your legs, and it doesn't feel as if a tiny army of angry leprechauns are running around inside your underwear and spanking you in a rage. And you start to forget how agonizing it was, how utterly out of body. The memories fade along with the scars, like that time you got beat up in third grade, or childbirth.

And then you catch it in the mirror.

And it is so goddamned cute.

And you are hooked.

Now that I get regular bikini waxes, I wish everyone else would too. Whenever I catch a woman at the beach smuggling what appears to be a cluster of kittens in the bottom of her "swim dress," or some guy strutting down the streets with a ferretlike growth emerging from the front of his 1975 school-district-issued gym short shorts, I wish it were mandatory. The more you get them, the less painful they are, and the better you get at making the uncomfortable "I know and you know that you are dangerously close to the little lady down there so let's both talk about where we're going for summer vacation" talk. And the cuter and cuter you are naked. The bikini wax isn't something I do for guys, or even for other girls. This is purely for me, so that when I get out of the shower in the morning (oh, who am I kidding, the late afternoon), and I stand in the mirror and do that once-over visual inventory that we all do right before we mentally slap ourselves and think *Stop picking yourself over! You're a beautiful creature of god!*, I can think, *Man, that thing sure is cute.*

The first time I did it, I did feel a little rueful afterward, even guilty—kind of like the first time you tweeze your eyebrows and you stare at your raw, reddening temple and wonder, for a moment, whether having lounging fat caterpillars on your face was somehow better than the sparse line of languorous fleas weaving uneasily across your forehead now. Much of our modern grooming ritual is about removing stuff that nature put there to protect us—the caveman us, anyway—from our surroundings: ear wax (keeps beetles from crawling in your ear and nibbling on your ear drum—that would suck); toenails (keeps your tootsies from being stubbed on a boulder as you chase down a woolly mammoth); eyebrow hair (keeps prehistoric crap from falling into your eyes and blinding you while you're trying to run away from a hungry saber-toothed tiger); and body hair (keeps you warm when your caveman has stolen all the skins in the middle of the night and you're forced to sleep on the hard, cold stone floor of the cave, even though snow and ice are blowing through the cave opening and that lazy motherfucker refused to get any more wood for the fire and now it's cold as a polar bear's ass in there). Thankfully, due to science and progress and good ol' extinction, we don't need any of that stuff anymore. But what purpose do the shorties serve? Camouflage? Insulation? Keeping bits of lunch from falling onto your delicates? I have no idea. And anyway, we have the thong for all that now.

The bikini wax is a gateway treatment, much in the same way that pot is a gateway drug. You go in, thinking very utilitarian thoughts, about how this is a luxury but you *have* to have it because you're going to be on a beach, or at a pool, or in a fraternity basement filled with sand, *around other people* for chrissake, and it would be rude not to take off a little around the sides. But once you have decided that the wax is something you must have, the glorious, aromatherapy-oiled slide down the slippery slope begins. I now believe very deeply in regular maintenance. *Deeply.* I think you could forgo all of the frosting—the eye shadows and the hairsprays and the fluffing and preening and pouting and lining—if you just spent a little time and energy doing basic maintenance. To wit:

A regular pedicure

I am telling you, of all the things I have seen guys go crazy over, the pedicure is number one. Guys may want to hump a girl with big boobs,[9] but they immediately begin falling in love when they see a girl with a gorgeous set of toes. I have had boys point, and squawk, and punch their friends, and ask me to wait while they get people from the other room, to take a look at my toes. Mind you, my toes are nothing special. They're normal, human toes.[10] They're just well maintained. And this is not an expensive proposition. Save up your money, and find a great little nail shop in your area where they do the quick cheap jobs, like a "Mini Nails" or a "Paradise Ten Salon for Nails" or a "Miki's Quikis." Don't forget to bring your own set of nail tools. Some places are not so in love with "the hygiene" and the last thing you want is to get the last girl's toeness all mixed up with your toeness; that's a good way to end up toeless (punny!). Get a great pedicure once a month, then do your own touchups. You can do it. I believe in you. Of course a spa pedicure is much better and, if you can afford it, say, by giving up regular meals or selling some blood, go for it.

9. Yes, I *am* sophisticated.
10. Boys love nice toes. It's just a fundamental truth. They are a peculiar species. By the way, if there is a boy reading this, you should get a pedicure too. It doesn't have to be all girly, with colors 'n' stuff. It can be nice and masculine. Because guess what? Girls like a nice set of toes on a guy too. If they're clawlike and filthy, we'll ignore them, because that's how we do, but we'll talk about you mercilessly later with our friends. Hm-hm. Yup.

An occasional manicure

I am not such a stickler for a manicure, mainly because I am a great tall brute who chews her nails and uses them to pick safe locks and open beer bottles. An occasional one to keep you from looking like a coal miner is fine, or just keep them clean and file them so you don't look like you just dug your way out of your own grave. Again, these can be cheaply had at the nail shop around the way, or you can get together with your girlfriends and give them to each other, right before you have a pillow fight in your underwear and start making out. Wait, isn't that what we all do?

Regular waxing services

Despite my less than enticing description, I advocate regular leg and bikini waxes wholeheartedly. This would also be a good time to get your brows done, either waxed or plucked: pick your torture. I think nice, trimmed up brows, like a nice trimmed up you-know-what, are the quickest way to reveal how beautiful your eyes are, especially if they've been hiding behind an Andy-Rooneyesque unibrow. A regular wax job does three things: keeps you looking and feeling all silky smooth, which everybody likes—boys, girls, kittens, everyone; keeps you from cutting yourself all to hell with that stupid murder weapon on a stick they call a razor (I swear, they're out to kill me), and prevents you from suffering from excruciating itching and even more excruciating razor bumps (oh, you thought only guys got them?); and keeps you humble. You will have suffered for your beauty, which will keep you from developing any feelings of smugness or self-entitlement. You will know that these other women that you see, looking all golden and buttery smooth, also had their hindquarters abused by a sadist in a white coat with a stack of muslin strips. You will no longer feel inferior, but also no more superior, having suffered yourself. No one likes a snob.

A massage

This will make you feel more relaxed, more comfortable and in touch with your body, and will make you stand a little taller. Which will make you fly as hell.

A facial

I am not a huge fan of these, as I have very sensitive skin and break out when a butterfly's wings brush past my cheeks. But if you can find a nice, noninvasive, soothing, nourishing facial treatment, by all means, do it. Your skin is what's beautiful about you, not all the crap you heap on it. Facials can really help people who have difficult skin, and you can learn a lot about how to better take care of your face from a qualified facialist. From an unqualified facialist, you can learn how to get your face to break out completely in twenty-four hours or less, so don't go to someone unless one of your friends, who is not blotchy, lumpy, or blackened in any way, recommended her.

That's it. Take care of yourself and you won't have to do much else. It's deceptively simple, but brilliant.

Cue wicked evil scientist laughter.

The Sociocultural Significance of the Second Coming of Missy Elliott

I was watching this show on MTV called *Driven*, of which I've only seen like three episodes, but which only took that three episodes to convince me it was the most irrelevant documentary program on television.

Not because it's not riveting, because it is (it's like *Behind the Music*, only without the drug overdoses, beer guts, and scraggly facial hair), and not because it's not true documentary, because it's that as well (they actually talk to family members and old high-school teachers and business associates, and not to the documentary subject at all, which lends it that "true news" authenticity). It's irrelevant not because of its subject matter (which is big fat music stars and how they got to be big fat music stars) but because the show itself is its own self-fulfilling prophecy.

See, the topic of the show is the name of the show,

which is *Driven,* and the point of the show is to demonstrate how this singer or that rapper's intense motivation and commitment to the game got them to where they are now. But what massive recording artist isn't intensely motivated and completely committed? You have to be to have that kind of success—even the most preconstructed of juicy-pop boy bands is required to put in long hours and make grand personal sacrifices to succeed. I find it highly unlikely that you're going to find a show on MTV called *Lackadaisical and Insanely Fortunate,* where some joker with middling talent and a knack for sleeping fourteen hours a day suddenly goes quadruple platinum and sets off on an eleven-country world tour. If these people have made it, it is *because* they are driven. And so every one of these stories is how some scrappy young artist left home at a young age with nothing more than the clothes on their back and a few dollars and a can of beans in a hobo sack, came to the big city, had some initial success only to be smacked down, was plucky enough to push on in the face of indomitable odds, and came out on top. It's a good story, which is why it's so entertaining night after night.

My favorite so far is the one about Missy Elliott. I could give you the details, but they're pretty much what you just read. The most interesting part, however, was that in the beginning Missy was in a girl group. And she was the most curvy of the girls, and people kept pressuring her to lose weight. And she never beat herself up about it, or got her feelings hurt, or withdrew, or lashed out, or starved herself. She just told them, "Don't worry about my weight. My talent is going to make you forget all that." And they pooh-poohed her, or whatever it is that music people do (call you wack, diss you live on the VMAs, dangle you off a balcony by your feet), and she just kept plugging away, grilling up the hot beats. And when she put out her first album, and had a chance to do her first video, instead of having it shot in a way that made her look thinner, like all in closeups, or with digital retouching, or whatever, she actually chose to do it in a way that made her look even *bigger*. She put on all these rubber suits that they filled with air, making her look like a great round licorice button, and they shot some of it with a fishbowl lens, and she bounced around the sets like a big beautiful gumball. She emphasized the exact thing that people had told her all along would be the thing that would hold her back. She threw it right back in their face—*bam!* Oooh, that girl's got balls.

Of course, the end of the show you know. She's a big ol' multiplatinum star, and everyone wants a piece of Missy, and she's got a zillion endorsements and a jeans commercial and she's zaftig all the way to the bank. She makes all her own money, and all her own music, and all kinds of other people wish she would make all their music, too, and she rocks crazy custom outfits all made out of leather, a fabric that makes a lot of narrow-assed girls wake up in the night all sweaty and panicky and crying for their mamas. All of her music is lusciously, drippingly, agonizingly erotic, and she is a sexually aggressive woman, and she is hilarious with it, and she is wild and dirty and hardcore and people want her, and want to be her, and *want to get with that*.

What's confusing is that there is still this ongoing dialogue about the demand that girls in entertainment be rail thin. It's there, don't get me wrong, that whole beauty standard still exists, and it's real. But there are all these luscious, hippy, puffy, thick women running around, being sexual and commanding and free and oh-so-fucking cool, and we admire them. We admire Missy and J.Lo and Jill Scott and Natalie Maines and Macy Gray and Beyoncé (I also have to admit that I have a bit of a girl crush on English TV cook Nigella Lawson, who is like a Botticelli painting in an apron, always licking whipped cream or custard off spoons and fingers). We think they are cool and beautiful and talented and taking care of business and completely and utterly fly—so why don't we see ourselves in them when it comes to our incessant desire to be stick ladies on stilts?

I was in New York once, visiting with a couple of male friends of mine, one who had recently gotten in shape for a movie role. And the guy was supercut, no joke. The guy was shredded. You could see his heart beating and his liver converting sugar to energy right through his stomach, the guy was so fat-free. I was duly impressed, and began grilling him, because I wanted to lose some weight and get really cut too. And both guys immediately looked stricken. They began yelling at me, interrupting each other, the words tumbling out in a panic, all protestations and admonitions, clamoring to be heard, insistent, angry, even. And what they both said was "Noooo! Don't do that! Don't lose weight! Guys like curves!" And from the look on their faces, you could tell they weren't just talking to me. They were talking to women all over the country; indeed, all over the world. *Guys like curves.*

Look at porn actresses and strippers. They are all curvy, hips and buttocks and cheeks like a plump newborn. Hell, look at the girls at Hooters. Those nylon shorts must have the tensile strength of a suspension bridge cable, because the seams are under constant threat of bursting from the pressure. I have a lot of guy friends, and to a man, and I mean this, *to a man,* they all say they would rather date a girl with curves.

The love of a curvy girl is even more prevalent now with the dominance of hip hop in pop culture. As annoying as the bitches-on-parade videos can be (as in, "That dude had eighty fine bitches in his video, so I got to have a hundred! No, two hundred! And a Bentley made of *gold!*"), there is a lot to be learned from them. The women in these videos, and there are a lot, are always curvy. Round and plump and soft, with bottoms creeping up out of low-cut jeans and down out of hot pants. They are hippy and soft and luscious, and they are all half-naked with no psychic scars from things rolling over or spilling out or folding in, indeed, with no apparent emotional repercussions at all. They are *happy* to be hippy and soft and luscious, and the guys with them are even more happy about it than they are. They rap about it. They sing about it. They make up new words for it, like *phat* and *thick* and *trunk* and *double-wide*. All of which are good things to them. Great things. Things that elicit praise like "I like it when you do that right thurr" and anguished curses of "Damn them jeans!" So, why do we still all want to have asses like a thirteen-year-old Japanese gymnast? Why do we still think it would be better to look as if we just recovered from a six-month-long bout with an intestinal parasite?

Guys. Like. Curves. So why is it that girls don't?

I think there are strong, powerful, and lingering ideas of what we think we *should* be, that fight every day in our heads with what we know we *can* be. I think we still believe being superthin is being powerful, is being in control, is being smarter, more creative, more productive, better. But as Missy so pointedly and deliciously points out, it's not. Not even a little bit.

Rock your body

Sometimes I get up in the morning and I just want to poke myself in the eye. Really. Just take an index finger and poke myself in my lefty.

I have this routine, and it's a routine I enjoy, and I hate myself for enjoying it, but feelings are feelings and what can I do? But occasionally, I just get disgusted with the whole thing and I want to put a pinky right in my socket and be done with it. Here is the routine. I get up in the morning, usually much later than I had planned. Every night I go to bed and I think, "Tomorrow I'm going to get up really early. I'm going to read the paper front to back, every article, and really read it this time, not just look at the photos and little color graphs. And then, with all I've learned, I'm going to come up with a way to end world hunger, and email that to Kofi Annan at the United Nations, for which he'll be eternally grateful, and will submit me for the Nobel Prize. Then I'll read one of the world's great novels, have some fiber cereal, and go spend the morning with the homeless down at the mission. I'll tell them all about my plan for ending world hunger, starting with them, and they'll be so overwhelmed with joy that the schizophrenics will become lucid, the lame will walk, and that one hobo with the single, giant dreadlock will grab a pair of scissors and cut it off, donating it to science. Yes . . . that's it. Up at four. Tomorrow's the day . . ."

I wake up at nine-thirty. My plans for saving the world are dashed. Instead, I get up and do a bunch of things so awfully Hollywood that if I saw someone else doing them I'd want to hit them with a skateboard. I stumble out of bed, put on workout clothes, drink both a soy drink *and* an energy drink, and go to the gym. Me, me, me, it's all about me. The shame. The eye-poking shame.

The embarrassing thing is, I love going to the gym. I love it. I am one of those assholes you see on the treadmill, skipping and leaping away, running at some gawdawfully unnatural speed, completely disregarding the little laminated sign that says *Hey Friends! Share the Fun! Twenty minutes per workout on the aerobic machines please!*, ignoring the glares and teeth sucking and towel snapping from the line of people forming behind her. Occasionally, I get a glimpse of myself in the glass doors of the spinning studio as one of those poor rubes comes stumbling out, gingerly rubbing that special spot between their mistreated cheeks, wincing ruefully, and I think, *Who is that jackass hogging the treadmill? Doesn't she have anything better to do with her time?* And then I realize, *Hey! That jackass is me!*

The problem is, working out kicks ass. It is completely addictive and the number one thing you can do to make yourself happier, more beautiful, healthier, stronger, smarter, and generally cooler than everyone else you know. People do a lot of other things to accomplish the above. They drink, they smoke, they do drugs of varying provenance, both prescription and black market. They have sex with strangers. They have sex with friends. They have sex with strange friends. They starve themselves, gorge themselves, make themselves disgorge. They eat only grapefruit and become anemic, then eat only meat and become lethargic (and develop mind-boggling halitosis). They are mean to people they love and nice to people they hate. They pay thousands and thousands of dollars for a doctor to slice into their flesh, stab them with needles, jab them with giant metal tubes until their torsos fill with fluid, and their kidneys break down.

They join cults. They pursue money. They pray for money. They meditate on money. They steal money. They steal money from their cults while everyone else is meditating.

And guess what?

None of this makes them any smarter, more beautiful, more lovable, younger, or happier. But forty minutes on a treadmill every day would. It would do all of those things and more. And it would save them from going to prison for stealing money from the meditating cult members, where they would have to work out like the dickens to avoid looking like tender, young fresh fish to Big Poppa Jones and Meathook in the next cell.

I am not a workout guru. I do not believe in the all-encompassing power of exercise. I am not going to jump off of a trampoline and into your living room, legwarmers blowing in the wind, butt-floss leotard in permanent camel-toe formation, squawk, "Stop the Insanity!"[11] then tearfully relate how aerobic step-ball jazzercise changed my life, increased my bra size, and stopped the aliens from communicating with me through my television set.[12] A workout is a workout. It's sweaty and difficult and mildly excruciating and a big fat pain in the ass. But every time I leave the house to go to the gym I feel like crap. And every time I

11. Remember Susan Powter, the buzzcut diminutive blonde jumping bean of an exercise guru who, for a couple of years in the late nineties, could be seen on virtually every daytime talk show on TV? No? Me neither.

12. I'm not implying that aliens communicated with Powter. I have no idea if they were. But it sure would have explained a lot.

59

leave the gym to go home I feel like the Pink Power Ranger. Compare that to the feeling I have when I leave a bar after fourteen lycheetinis, which usually hovers between overwhelming regret, the hot prickly flush of shame and *oh my god I have to puke so badly I don't think I can puke . . . wait a minute here it comes.*

I'm not advocating that you be razor thin, or pencil thin or even dill-pickle thin. Hell, be meatball-hoagie thick if you like. You should be whatever feels good to you. But there is nothing sexier, nothing more radiant and captivating, than a woman who's just worked her body to the point of glisten and beyond. No makeup, hair looking like someone stuck her head in a public toilet and kicked the handle, listing to one side like a scuttled pirate ship because, once again, she blew off the stretching (too much of a drag). That woman is beyootiful. Gorgeous. I have seen guys double up like a broken theater seat when a sweaty, panting, flushed woman passes by in bicycle shorts and a man's T-shirt covered in a Jackson Pollock of her own makeup. Why? Because a) that woman looks like she just had sex, b) because that woman looks like she's got the stamina to have great sex, and c) because that woman takes care of her body, and thusly has a body built for . . . the great sex.

Back to the thinness thing. I need to say, first of all, that looking at celebrities, people in the television and film business, as role models is a big fat waste of time. Not that you shouldn't look at these women as inspiration—we all need to have something to aspire to. But to look at Giselle Bündchen and think, *Man, all I need to do is lose ninety pounds and get a killer bikini wax and I am going to have her beat!* is just plain dunderheaded. Women like Giselle are unnatural, flukes of nature, genetic misfirings that alternately produce people with feet growing out of their backs or supermodels. Most people in the entertainment business are highly unusual. They're born with a unique set of physical circumstances, and then they make it their business to keep those circumstances looking as good as they can. It's their *job* to be thin. *Their job.* Actresses and models being thin is like a secretary being able to type. It's a prerequisite for the job. Yes, secretaries who can't type probably still get work, but they better make one hell of a Xerox copy. Public attitudes and mores are changing, and they should, because these bodies just aren't real. They aren't real. So admire them, aspire, envy, throw darts, make voodoo dolls and pin-the-tail-on-the-emaciated-waif posters, but don't try to be like them. The fact of the matter is that you can be fly as hell without being a size six.

Looking fly, feeling fly, is about looking and feeling healthy and strong. It is not about eliciting winces of pain from the guys and winces of disgust from the girls every time you walk through a room. Working out makes you healthy, makes you strong, gives you the kind of physical strength you need to make it through a long night of partying without fainting like a nineteenth-century courtier and the kind of self-confidence to tell all the people around you, when they are telling you there is no way you will ever be a huge multiplatinum hip-hop artist (or great chef, or cat fancier, or high-altitude oxygen-free mountain climber, whatever floats your junk) to go screw themselves.

I am not even going to presume to tell you what you should do. Good lord, hon, figure that out for yourself. I'm not a trainer. Join a gym. Take a yoga class. Try to learn how to play golf. Poke the next door neighbor's dog in the eye with a stick and then try to get away before it tears your fibula off. Like I said, I am not an exercise guru.

But I *do* want you to stop the insanity.

The Uppity Bitch Paradox

or

Who the F**k You
Calling Sassy?

I have a problem with my mouth.

I have always had this problem. It's not a mechanical problem. And it's not gingivitis, or overactive salivary glands, or a quivering lower-lip tic that makes people wonder whether I've had a stroke.[13] My mouth, as an organ, and as an instrument, has always worked just fine. And that's the problem. It works a bit *too* well. Not that I'm saying I'm some kind of verbal genius or wordsmith or anything. I'm not claiming to have a brilliant mouth, just a prolific one. A productive one. One that churns out a million words a minute, oftentimes the wrong ones, and always at the worst possible time.

---

13. Which is something I've wondered often about Greta Van Susteren, even after the massive facial overhaul. Why it matters, I don't know. The mind wants to know unimportant things sometimes.

One of people's favorite questions for a comedian is, "Were you always funny? Were you a class clown?" Which I don't understand, because a) what does it matter, really? You don't ask a mechanic if he used to take his Hot Wheels apart when he was a kid, or whether a doctor dissected his neighbor's cat and then tried to resuscitate its little kitty heart, do you? And b) I have always understood the word *clown* to be a bad word, a pejorative term, as in "I'm watching C-SPAN's coverage of the Senate Finance Committee. What a bunch of *clowns*." Or "I got dragged to an Adema concert last night. It was a total *clown* show." The term *class clown* conjures up images of that weird kid from the seventh grade who would spit loogies into the air and catch them back in his mouth, or threaten to wipe his boogers on other people, or unzip his Tuffskin corduroys, reach inside, stick his index finger through and then bob through the classroom wiggling it at all the girls when the teacher had stepped out into the hallway. He smelled like peanut butter and a little bit like pee, and when he put on his sweats for gym class he always seemed to have a half-mast chubby going. I did not want to be the class clown. The class clown was a *clown*.

No, I was not the class clown when I was younger. What I was, was a talker.

I talked in class. Constantly. Out of turn, unbidden, unrequited, unheard—it didn't matter to me. I was a gabbler. I talked to the teacher. I talked to my neighbors. I talked to myself. I made paper finger puppets and *they* talked to *themselves*. I was a conversationalist, dammit, a verbalizing machine. I would correct the teacher in mid-lecture, yell out answers, tag people's show-and-tell stories. I didn't care. My mouth had a mind of its own. It could not be stopped.

When I was young, the remedy was simple. Throw me out of class. I estimate that I only spent about forty percent of the second, third, fourth, sixth, ninth, and tenth grades actually in class. I was constantly in the hallways of my grade school, sitting on the floor, hanging out by the water fountain, making conversation with the janitor, waving at other students as they entered and exited the bathrooms, or running Dittos back and forth from the principal's office. (Yes, I was alive during the waning days of Dittos. It was a heady time.) I was there so much I got to be a fixture. Kids stopped teasing me and started respecting me—it was like the end of *Rudy*, where everyone had to respect the kooky kid for gutting it out, as pathetic as it seemed. I was the Rudy of my grade school, always bumming about the hallways, counting the minutes until I could get back inside the classroom and finally prove to everyone that I had the ability to control my big mouth. Of course I didn't, and I'd be out in the hallway during the next period, the scenario finally too familiar to be shameful, cheerfully giggling with the kid from the next class over who'd been put out for smooshing paste in another kid's hair.

My report cards were always the same: "Aisha is bright

and intelligent, but needs to apply herself more in class. She is disruptive and talkative; she distracts the other children and can't seem to focus on the work at hand. She has a clear problem with authority and when reprimanded, she is insubordinate. She is *sassy* toward the teachers." That was the first time I encountered the word *sassy*. It seemed like a bad thing to be, a putdown, an insult. "Miss Sassypants!" "Don't get sassy with me!" "Sass me again and I'll give you something to sass about!"[14] I didn't like it then, and I don't like it now.

When I got to high school, the problem got worse. I had been at a relatively laidback, kind of modern philosophy grade school, where we called the teachers by their first names and did a lot of hugging. My fourth-grade music class consisted entirely of a hippie lady in a dirndl skirt and clogs who came to school twice a week to teach us revolutionary folk songs in an effort to jumpstart another generation of young American radicals; all she succeeded in doing is making us hate acoustic guitar. Despite the fact that I was constantly being disciplined, that discipline usually came in the form of some quiet time in the hallway, or some quiet time in the principal's office, or some quiet time making Dittos while everyone else was outside playing tetherball. It was all pretty benign and soft-boiled. But by the tenth grade my parents got sick of paying for me to have long, heated existential conversations in the hallway

14. This one never seemed to make sense to me, either.

with the school janitor like some junior David Thewlis, and they moved me into a public school. I may as well have been sent to a Siberian gulag.

Public school was mean. It was corporal. It was meant to manage and contain and suppress—education was completely secondary. You were not allowed to have an original thought, or express an alternative perspective, or disagree with anyone, let alone the teacher. And goddamn it, before you speak, before you move, before you even think, you had better *raise your fucking hand!*

You can see what kind of a problem this would pose for me.

Nurtured by the hippie cocoon of my grade school, and bolstered by my family's get-up-and-go philosophy,[15] I had started to take my own ideas very seriously. And it was absolutely critical to me that I be able to express them freely to others. This is why the practice of having to raise your hand was so utterly distasteful to me. I had something important to say, and I needed to say it, and I did not want to wait until Mr. Crumpetjammer or whoever deigned to grant me the honor of addressing the group. It

15. Every morning before I left for school, my dad would give me a rousing pep talk, the upshot of which was usually "Get out there and grab life by the balls and yank down hard! And don't have sex with boys." Or something like that. I realize it may seem inappropriate for a father to use the word balls with his teenage daughter, but my dad is a no-nonsense kind of guy. I knew he meant it metaphorically. Because really, life doesn't have testicles, now does it?

was demeaning and archaic and, what's more, it hurt my arm. How long did these people expect you to keep your limb aloft? What was I, a Jedi? I would hold it erect, then switch arms, then back again, then fold one over my head and wrap it around the other one for support, then make my left elbow into a little brace that I would wedge against my desk to buoy up the right, which by this time was pointing straight forward, hand drooping like a wounded bird. I would sigh loudly, tap my feet, roll my eyes, squeak, grunt, do *anything* I could to get this blockheaded teacher to see that *I had something very important to say!* What were these people, blind? Very well, then. I would resort to the old ways. The old ways were always better. That was what my grandmother always said, and she was always right, except when she told me that my face would freeze that way, and the time she bought me enormous belted pads when I got my first period. But, other than that, she was spot on. I went back to speaking out, and back to spending large chunks of time in face-to-face encounters with middle-aged people in scratchy, off-brand suits.

My problem with speaking out became a full-blown affliction. And it was starting to pay off. Sort of. I was getting kind of famous (bad famous, not good famous)[16] for get-

---

16. Despite our country's overwhelming obsession with fame, being famous is not always a good thing. Just ask Monica Lewinsky, who's famous for giving a very sloppy blow job, or Dan Quayle, who's famous for being dumb, or the Spice Girls, who . . . oh, never mind.

ting in fights—verbal ones, but fights nonetheless (don't diminish my sense of self-importance)—with teachers. I was becoming legendary for mouthing off, and then mouthing off again, and then *arguing*, with my superiors. Not once, or twice, but many, many times. I don't know how it happened—it wasn't as if I set out to be the classroom asshole—it just kind of happened.

I guess the whole problem originated with the fact that I felt that school was demeaning, that the teachers didn't want to be there, and that they didn't even make a half-hearted, rudimentary effort to hide that from the students. They came late, showed movies, bribed kids with candy, gave out seventh grade–level work to eleventh-grade students, were corporal in instances that didn't demand it and lackadaisical when students were fornicating and stabbing each other in the neck in the back of the classroom. It kind of pissed me off.

Of course, there were exceptions. Lots of them. I had some kickass teachers in high school, some real winners. They were smart, and motivated, and they really wanted their students to learn. They came in early, and stayed late, and weren't so fearful of the nation's wasted youth that they refused to have a conversation with you outside of the (relatively) safe context of the security-guard–filled campus. They would take phone calls at home, and host study groups on the weekend, and didn't stare you down imperiously when you asked a question that couldn't be answered from a prescribed list of retorts provided in the study guide that came from the textbook publisher. These people were awesome. They restored my faith in humanity. They kept me from hating school. They kept me from hating life.

But the rest of them . . .

The biggest fight I ever had with a teacher, the one that made me famous (at my school, anyway), happened my junior year. I can't remember the teacher's name, or even what class she taught, mainly because she was *so* completely unmemorable. As a teacher, she was ineffectual and nondescript, and she insisted on teaching from a teacher's guide rather than from the books that the students actually had to go through the trouble of reading. I began to suspect, as the semester wore on and it seemed she couldn't respond to a query without consulting her trusty teacher's guide (which by this time had started to resemble the Shroud of Turin, it was so thumbed through), that maybe she didn't know the material, that maybe she hadn't read it herself. Once this idea entered my head, it was impossible to shake. And the more I watched her fumble and rattle and hem and procrastinate, rifling anxiously through answer sheets and workbook legends and the dusty card catalog of her spotty memory, the angrier I got. And the angrier I got, the more I would pepper her with questions—complex, annoying, unanswerable questions—in the hopes of completely stumping the chump. And the more the chump was stumped, the more she would ignore me, until I would have my hand up for the duration of the class, obstinate and enraged, and she would look the other way for the duration of the class, obstinate and dumb.

Yes, fine. I do realize that I had a problem with authority. I resented having to wait to be told when it was time to express my opinion, that what I had to say was only valuable when someone else said it was. And I especially resented those admonitions when they came from someone who didn't seem to know a goddamn thing she hadn't read somewhere else first. I had been raised to be outspoken, a free thinker, an expressive. It was too late for me to change then. And it's too late for me now. I have a big fat mouth.

Finally, one day I just exploded. (I'm not proud of it. It just happened.) I asked her some question (probably just to be difficult—at this point, I had resigned myself to not getting an A, or even a C), and she couldn't answer it without going to that dogeared fucking handbook, and I just blurted, "Don't you know *anything*?"[17] The yelling match that followed was unprecedented in that school district (or any other, I imagine), in that it stayed mostly in the realm of the academic, and didn't include the phrases "kiss my ass," or "you can't suspend me, my father's the principal," or "I'm gonna cut you, teacher lady." She eventually did manage to throw me out of class, and I huffed down the

17. Yes, in retrospect, I was a shit.

hallway to the principal's office, fully prepared to defend myself, with charts and graphs and quotations, as well as quite a few crocodile tears.

Then something miraculous happened. I *didn't* get in trouble. The principal—who by this time had a pretty good sense of who I really was, that I didn't carry a gun, or a mixture of Cherry Coke and Pusser's Rum in a flask in my backpack,[18] and that I did all my homework, got generally good grades, and didn't plan to blow the school up or start a knife-fight-slash-dance contest in the courtyard between rival ethnic gangs—simply told me I needed to manage my temper, and know when it was appropriate to speak up and when it was appropriate to bite my tongue, but that I was inquisitive and academically demanding and he couldn't fault me for wanting more out of my educational experience. And then he transferred me out of the dumb lady's class. (And soon after that, she disappeared. Hah.)

And that was when I learned (after I recovered from the head injury sustained when I fainted from shock) that speaking up, being *sassy*, was a good thing.

I still didn't like the word, and I still don't. Because somehow, despite the fact that what it describes is good stuff—being outspoken, honest, forthright, incisive—it

18. There was actually a guy in my school who did this, and would give out swigs during homeroom. He was *extremely* popular, but not such an ace in the classroom.

somehow still reminds me of those times when I would get in trouble as a kid, and be told that "a sassy mouth means a soft behind."[19] It's a word you use with a little girl, a preteen descriptor, a way of dismissing an opinionated woman's ideas. Instead of calling her intelligent or articulate, you call her *sassy*. Which immediately calls to mind prepubescence. I mean, they named a magazine for pre-teens *Sassy*. Somehow that says it all.

The word *lively*, as well as *brassy, brazen, feisty*, and *spitfire*, all seem to me to be words that guys in bad action movies use to describe some barmaid or pizza waitress or drunken archaeologist in a Mongolian bar, right before they try to bang her. As in, "mmm, *she's* feisty" (lick lips, smirk lecherously, cut to hot sex underneath a mosquito net). They are little words, words of aspersion, and I don't like 'em. (I do, however, like the word *foxy*. I realize that has nothing to do with what I've been talking about, but it's a hot word and it should come back into the popular lexicon immediately.)

I don't like words like *sassy* mainly because there are no corresponding words for guys. You would never call a dude *feisty*. He would punch you in the mouth. Guys are *supposed* to speak their minds. They're supposed to mouth off. That's why there's no descriptor for the guy who does it. Because they *all* do it. Guys are born to be brassy.

19. I *always* knew what that meant!

They're socialized to be brazen. That's their birthright. We, somehow, have to earn it.

To which I say a hearty *fuck that*.

I think girls should make being sassy, or brazen, or feisty, or loudmouthed, or audacious, or brash, or impudent, or any of the other double entendre tidbits that are used to dismiss girls that are just sticking up for themselves and speaking their minds, the normal state of things. We shouldn't feel empowered to speak out, because it should just be the way we are, *how we do*. I've been lucky enough to turn my big mouth into a vocation, and I don't think anything of popping off a well-placed retort when it's warranted. I still speak out of turn, I tag other people's conversations, and I am an awful interrupter. (I am working on it though; really, that's just rude!) I play in a regular poker game with a bunch of guys, during which I repeatedly call them "my beeyotch"—this is usually said in a high-pitched Snoop Dogg voice, followed by a slamming down of a full house and a lot of cackling and rolling around in a pile of money. I especially enjoy doing that.

Being outspoken doesn't mean being mean. It just means knowing yourself, and what you deserve, and when it's time to ask for it. Finding the strength to express your ideas and desires and opinions forces you to figure out what your ideas and desires and opinions *are*. And doing that gets you on a path to getting more of what you want out of your own life. Because you can't start getting what you want if you haven't figured out what that is, and you might not bother to figure out what that is, if you've never had to tell anyone about it. You might just go bobbing about, never speaking up, knowing you were uncomfortable with the way things are, but not really understanding why, until one day you explode like a big walking blob of C4 at the mailman, or your boyfriend, or your boss, or (god forbid) your teacher.

Action is actualization. Doing is making real. So say what you think. Be outspoken. Be bold. Be articulate. Be sarcastic. Be silly, even. Get your shots in.

But for gawd's sake, just don't call it *sassy*.

The Ballad of Yogurt Girl

I vowed that, no matter what, I would never become the yogurt girl.

I had a job, when I first got out of college, in an office. And it was a typical office, with cubicles and low-pile, stain-resistant carpet, and a guy who delivered mail from a little cart with wheels. And it had conference rooms that smelled like cold cuts, because cold cuts would often be left out in those conference rooms after whatever meeting that required cold cuts in order to occur had ended.

This company had a lot of young people working there, young, hungry people, most of whom were poor, one of whom was me. These young, hungry people lived at that office: came in early, worked late, toiled away on weekends, slept in empty offices, drank beer at their desks when they thought no one was looking. They were hungry, and they were poor, and they were overworked and underpaid, and goddamn it, they were going to get drunk at work because they deserved it.

This underclass of young, hungry people were scavengers. Because they all made just enough money to pay their rent, college loan installments, and monthly bus pass, there was nothing left over for food. These people went to work every day in a beautiful high-rise building, but they were all starving as hell. And so they became resourceful. Since I was one of them, so did I.

This resourcefulness took many forms, but the most prevalent, and productive, was the "post-office-event swoop." Because this was a pretty successful company, with lots of money to burn on flower arrangements and cocktail parties and catering (but, apparently, not enough to burn on entry level salaries), there was always food at every meeting. *Every* meeting. Client presentations, internal staff meetings, performance reviews. No matter the subject matter or size of the group, you could be sure there would be a giant plastic platter of halved marble muffins, a bowl of room temperature fruit salad, or a jumble of brownies and cookies, set out by the hapless assistant of whatever bigwig was running the meeting.

These hapless, starving, overworked, flirting-with-the-edge-of-scurvy assistants were a part of a network of such hapless folk, all of whom had a system. Whatever number of people the boss said would be in the meeting, the order for food placed would always be for at least twice that. Six people in the meeting, focaccia sandwiches for twelve. Training seminar for twenty, fifty sourdough bowls it is. Senior level tête-à-tête, cookies for a refugee camp. A mid-level executive's birthday always commanded a full celebration, replete with coffee, ice cream, champagne, and a sheet cake that could have ended world hunger. This strategy ensured that there were always ample leftovers for the roving packs of hungry young assistants and junior executives hovering outside of meetings and presentations, waiting for the older executives to disperse. As soon as a meeting adjourned, a call would go out, just a whisper at first, a murmuring among the reeds. Slowly, slowly, the murmur would grow into a babble and hum, and finally a verbal siren call—"Bagels in Conference 2! Bagels *and cream cheese* in Conference 2! Hurry before all the lox are gone!" And the hordes would descend like a swarm of carrion crows, piling baked goods and orange quarters, turkey slices and brownie triangles onto paper plates, Styrofoam bowls, paper towels snatched from the bathroom, or into the fronts of their dress shirts, held up to form little pouches, looking like futuristic marsupials—god damn the stains, this was war—fingers sticky, chins dripping, cheeks puffed out with whatever morsels were too small to bother wrapping up and taking home.

If you were alert, heartless, and unafraid to throw a couple of well-placed elbow jabs, you could be first through the door every time. The resourceful peon could live for weeks on what was scooped up in these free-for-alls. This was a way of life, and it was a good one. I lived almost exclusively on a diet of "everything" bagels, instant hot cocoa, chocolate chunk brownies, and open-faced focaccia sandwiches. Those were glorious days.

As I was poor, in debt up to my eyeballs (what maniac gives an eighteen-year-old a Visa card when the J. Crew catalog is so very, *very* handy?) and living off the grace of others, I was, as one might suspect, obsessed with food. Most of America is obsessed with food, and I'm not just talking women. Americans, as a whole, male and female, are obsessed, consumed, wholly focused at practically every minute of the day on what they are going to eat, what they have eaten, what they wish they could eat, what they can afford to eat, and how much they can get to eat for the least amount of money possible. Our news programs have segments on how to make bread pudding and hot wings and deep-fried Twinkies.[20] We are seduced by gimmicks (McSalad Shakers? C'mon!), drawn in by frosting, overwhelmed with portion size. We want snack packs and minibites and make-your-own-strudel swirls and wings that don't have bones and ice cream that has other ice cream buried inside it, and then inside of that, a ball of uncooked cookie dough. *Why would we want that?* We have

20. How is that news? A deep-fried Twinkie should be cause for national alarm—cops should be sent to the studio to break things up and cart the murderous inventor of this offense against humanity to jail. Why don't we just deep-fry a ball of lard and serve it with a nice crème anglaise?

no idea. We don't know why it's absolutely critical that our French fries be served to us in an urn rather than just a nice sensible bucket, or that our burger have six slices of bacon instead of a relatively spartan four. We just know that it's better that way, that that's the way it should be. I suppose, perhaps, that we want it that way because we can.

Add the very basic all-American obsession with food to the thirty or forty or one hundred food obsessions that the average American woman develops by the time she's oh, say, fourteen. Top that off with the kind of coal-fire-in-a-turret character in *Rent* poverty enjoyed by the recent college graduate, and you have a person whose every waking moment is spent contemplating edible matter and its centrality to the continuing function of her universe.

I thought about food constantly.

Part of this obsession included looking to see what other people were eating. During the course of my day I would cruise past the other peons' desks, casually inquiring after their bowl of udon noodles or deep dish slice or, on the days when I had something really good for lunch (my showstopper was homemade pizza, which I was quite proud of, because it looked expensive but cost about $1.67 to make and I could make two homemade pies last at least eight days) I'd make a point of eating it where other people could compliment me on my resourcefulness and gourmet savoir faire. In the afternoons, I'd peep in the public kitchen to see if there was any birthday cake (there almost always was—if you paid enough attention to the janitorial and security staff, you could find a reason to order birthday cake every day of the year), and take a gander in the community refrigerator to see whether there was a cheese plate that had escaped my eye. And so it was that I met yogurt girl.

Yogurt girl brought her lunch every day. Yogurt girl never scavenged. I didn't know yogurt girl because yogurt girl didn't move in my circle. She didn't like muffins and cake, brownies and ham. She did not like them, Sam I Am. She brought her lunch every day, and she ate it every day. And that was all she ate, day in and day out. And what yogurt girl brought for lunch every day . . . was yogurt.

One carton of yogurt. That's it. Every day. One. Carton. Yogurt.

She put it in the fridge, every day, in a plastic bag, with a spoon, so I knew that was all she brought. And I would see her retrieve the yogurt, then come back later, and primly dispose of the carton, and the spoon, and go back to her desk. I became fascinated with yogurt girl. *Fascinated.* Who was she? Why yogurt? Who could possibly survive a fourteen-hour day of typing and filing and being emotionally belittled by guys in tight gabardine on only one carton of yogurt? I, who felt as if I would faint if I didn't have some kind of baked good jammed half into my pie hole every hour on the hour, could not fathom it. But as much as I tried to learn her secret, catch her chugging chocolate milk or mainlining Tootsie Rolls at her desk, I finally had to admit that yogurt girl was some kind of machine, an automaton who could go for miles on one tiny sip of transmission fluid, which, in her case, was *yogurt*.

I sheepishly admit, being as young and stupid and malnourished as I was, that at first I admired yogurt girl. I admired her tenacity, her self-discipline, her single-mindedness. She didn't concern herself with mundane and unimportant matters like whether her food was delicious, or nutritious, or provided enough calories to keep her from swooning into her computer keyboard and ruining her PowerPoint presentation. No, she just ate that one little tiny yogurt, and went on about her business, never thinking about whether brownies and Cotto salami would make a good sandwich. She was free to use her time to think about important things, worky things, things that would get her ahead, get her to the point where she could actually afford to purchase food at the supermarket like real people. And she was thin. I would often look at yogurt girl, and think, "Man, I wish I was that thin. If I was that thin, I would be happy. I would have the love and adulation of others, become instantaneously smarter, solve the grand unified theory, become best friends with Stephen Hawking, and have fingernails that would finally grow longer than a shotputter's. I sure do wish I was yogurt girl. I bet yogurt girl's happy."

But as I watched yogurt girl, over lo, those many

months, she did not seem so happy. Yogurt girl did not smile much. Yogurt girl did not *glow*. Although yogurt girl couldn't have been more than twenty-three, she wore awful sweater sets and sensible pumps (the kind with the square heel and the comfort insoles) and was as gray as her Casual Corner skirt suit; she brushed her teeth in the bathroom obsessively (four times a day—I counted once) and never smiled at anyone. Yogurt girl did not have the love and adulation of others, I never saw her laughing, and I certainly never saw her drink beer at her desk when she thought no one was looking (which was my favorite thing to do and, once I got an officemate, became a regular Friday afternoon activity that ballooned into an unmanageable weekly riot that spilled far into the hallway and involved a pony keg of Old Milwaukee and an awful mixtape consisting primarily of MC Hammer and Pearl Jam, which is the musical equivalent of chocolate dipped in mustard). Despite repeated offers, we could never get yogurt girl to do a beer bong or pin the tail on the account supervisor or Stop! Hammer Time! Yogurt girl, despite all her discipline and love of cultured dairy, was miserable.

What's my point, besides the fact that a diet consisting entirely of yogurt makes you sad? It's that much of what we envy in another person, their thinness or their discipline or their ability to focus on work when others are having fun, isn't something we would really want, if pressed to examine it. That obsessing over what someone else is doing, having, being, feeling, getting, keeps us from enjoying what it is we're doing, having, being, feeling, getting. Or all the things we could be doing, having, being, feeling, getting. And eating.

Did I wish sometimes that I had eaten one less bagel, or spent five extra minutes on the treadmill, or had yogurt instead of a brownie turkey sandwich, or worked an extra hour instead of playing Quarters and Thumper on the floor in the reception area until I had to be scooped up, carried out, and placed on the train home?

Quite honestly, no. No, I didn't. We've got a finite amount of time on this planet, and I'll be damned if I'm not going to have a good time. It is your right, no, your responsibility, to enjoy your life, every bleeding tick-tocking morsel of it. Stay up late. Have an extra scoop of ice cream. Call in sick. Do not beat yourself up about these things. These things will not bring the planet to a halt. I'm not saying throw all common sense and restraint to the wind and take a bath in custard and Hennessy (although, *wow*, that sounds good). Discipline is good. Drive is good. Focus is good. It might be nice to have six-pack abs or a million bucks before you're thirty. But you're only young once. When you're old, and reflecting on your life over a mug of moonshine and some Melba toast, you won't think back to the time you did situps until you hurled. You'll think back to the time you sat up late with your friends, and played Mexicali until you hurled. And them right thar's golden memories.

* * *

Wherever she is, I hope yogurt girl has finally found happiness. Or at the very least diversified her diet a little, added a little fiber or something. All that yogurt's bound to bind you up. And that'll make anybody sad.

> SWERVE >

Once More in the Balls, with Feeling

I am a fan of the dirty joke. I do not have fragile sensibilities nor a delicate constitution. I do not faint, or wilt, or even swoon, in indelicate company. I will laugh at almost anything.

Loud burping, funny animal videos, guys getting hit in the nuts (which I think we should all finally admit as a group [we humans] is *always* funny, unless it's happening to a friend of yours, and then it's funny after they've fully recovered), people falling off of ladders, stories about bathroom mishaps (I am especially fond of ones where something incredibly awful happens in an extremely public place, and have been known to tell a few of those stories myself), baseball players bonking into stadium walls and each other, fart jokes, actual farting, kids hitting their dads in the head, knees or aforementioned crotch with wiffleball bats, footballs, Frisbees, rocks, or wooden sticks while in the process of trying to demolish a piñata.

I am a very easy laugh.

I don't know where it comes from—an innate desire to enjoy life perhaps, to find amusement in the small things as well as the monumental? Or maybe I'm just a blockhead with a fourth-grade sense of humor (which seems most likely). I dunno. Any way you slice it, I can laugh at almost anything. I've missed planes to very important meetings and fallen down on the floor in paroxysms, looking to all the world like a mental patient in dire need of an orderly and a sedative. I've laughed out loud in the middle of painful, tear-ridden breakups. Show me your serious, angst-ridden tragic play and I'll show you an hour and forty minutes of uncontrollable giggling. Part of this is compulsive, yes, but I do believe in the old "laugh to keep from crying" adage—the more things you can laugh about, the fewer things will send you racing for the pint of double chocolate-chip ice cream with the Zoloft topping.

And I don't much truck with dullards. Somber people skeeve me out. People who can't laugh at life, who peer at it through squinty, morose, judgmental eyes, are a pain in the ass. Pure and simple. They're a pain to themselves and a pain to the rest of us and they are much too much work to bother with. I reserve especial disdain for people that take themselves very seriously. Authors with tiny spectacles, tattooed guys who play bad guitar, blunt-smoking beat poets, the lady with the ring through her nose who works at the sex toy shoppe (they like to spell it that way; it makes them feel jaunty) and thinks she's a part of some great revolutionary movement rather than just a lady who helps people get their rocks off—good god, spare me the Cheshirelike self-satisfaction. It's exhausting.

If you are the president, a brain surgeon, that guy with the big headphones who looks concernedly at the computer screens as the space shuttle is taking off, or the pope, you are allowed to not have a sense of humor. Everyone else needs to lighten up. There is nothing cooler or sexier, more endearing or more powerful than a sense of humor. And we women tend to take ourselves way too seriously. We have had to work for so long and so hard to be taken seriously by others, that now we can't let a damn thing go! I mean really, if we can't laugh at ourselves, then who can we laugh at? Yes, we can laugh at guys, but even that gets old after a while. How many times can you laugh at a fart joke? And don't use me as a gauge—as I've said, fart jokes are my weakness.

Here's a case in point. A little while ago, I did a charity fund-raiser.

Wait—first of all, let me say that I love doing charity work. *Love* it. I say yes to charity events before I even know what they're for. "Raise money to save the pumpernickel bagel? Why sure!" "People for the Ethical Treatment of

~ AISHA TYLER ~

Prairie Dogs? Of course!" "The White Pants with Black Underwear Prevention Fund? Absolutely!" Philanthropy rocks.

Charity work is quite possibly the most fulfilling thing you can do with your time. In today's crazy, wealth-and-sex-obsessed, "My fake boobies are bigger than your fake boobies" world (or more accurately, "My horror story about my ruptured fake boobies is more devastating than your horror story about your liposuction procedure gone terribly awry"), volunteering still has meaning. It imparts value to what can otherwise be the pretty cavernous, rattletrap day to day. No matter how poor or down or bloated or lonely you feel, giving your time and energy to others brings you up. Now, before you huck the book across the room, banking it off the television and into your half-full laundry hamper, hooting "That's it! You can stuff your sanctimony in a sack, lady! I'm living in a studio apartment with a kitchenette the size of a postage stamp, eating Top Ramen and scrounging for old bus transfers so I can pay my college loans before I lose my last tooth!" I feel your pain. I am not trying to lecture. I am just saying it beats the hell out of sitting around your apartment on a Saturday, alphabetizing your CD collection and trying to figure out which pair of jeans makes your butt look flattest, or watching *Say Anything* for the four hundredth time. It is one of the coolest things I get to do, and I highly recommend it for five reasons:

1. **It's free.** For the low, low price of *nothing*, you get to enjoy hours and hours of fun helping others. They get food, or clothing, or affection, or learn how to read, or how to operate a voting booth (you'd think it'd be intuitive but apparently the entire state of Florida needs remedial classes), or whatever it is you've chosen to spend your time doing.

2. **It's easy.** What do you have to do, *really*? Show up in some schlubby clothes and hammer in a couple of nails? Hand out granola bars? Wear a hairnet? Someone else, much more dedicated and focused than you, has already done all the dirty work, organizing the workgroups and the clipboards and getting companies to donate juice boxes or tennis shoes or funds for experimental medical research, and setting up the card tables with the graham crackers and the pamphlets and the little folding chairs. All you have to do is show up and follow instructions. Come on, you GDI,[21] how bad can that possibly be?

3. **It's fulfilling.** So your job's not everything you imagined it would be. Instead of jet-setting from coast to coast, wooing powerful and wealthy clients over snifters of Armagnac and wowing high society with your pithy

21. God Damned Independent. A careful viewing of many excellent college comedies of the late nineties, including the fine film *PCU* starring Jon Favreau, will illuminate.

insights on pop culture, film, and American foreign policy in sub-Saharan Africa, you do alphanumerical filing in a damp, moldy cubicle and fetch highly aromatic taco salads for a boss who can barely tie her own shoes and accidentally locked herself inside the second-floor bathroom. Twice. So what? Drag your ass out on Saturday and do something that really matters. You will feel like you're actually making a difference in the world, the rest of your work life will seem less onerous, the other gray-faced sallow wage slaves in your cubicle sector will be awed by your compassion in the face of a soul-deadening workload, and the next time your boss locks herself in the bathroom and you take an hour to let her out, you can yawn, "I'm sorry I didn't rush to your aid, I was on the phone figuring out how the orphanage is going to get enough pairs of shoes for all of the sad, lonely *orphans*. I'm sorry, did you want me to get you a taco salad?"

4. **It's cool.** Because most of us are money-grubbing, self-aggrandizing junkyard dogs, people who do stuff out of the goodness of their hearts are as mysterious as Michael Jackson's nose (or lack thereof). You will enjoy the admiration and fear of others. And that, my friend, is a good feeling. Just ask the Rock.

5. **It makes you interesting.** The next time you're out with a bunch of people and they're all babbling on

about how their new SUV came with six cup holders instead of the standard factory-issue four, or how they're pissed because they couldn't find a pair of Super Humanity Force Five Superlow Cut Frayed Über-Denim jeans, you can talk about how you spent a weekend building a house for a low-income family and learned how to use a compound mitre saw. In *metric*. They will be cowed. But they will also be fascinated. Girls will think you've got balls, and boys will imagine you with a hammer in your hand, wearing nothing but a utility belt. Everybody wins.

Alright, enough of the lecture. The charity show I did was for *Ms.* magazine—an annual show they do every year in New York to raise money for the *Ms.* Foundation for Women, which, I think, provides money for new scratchy wool suits and fresh scowls of fury for young feminists everywhere.[22] Anyway, being a postmodern girl myself, I thought, "Great! I'll get to do some stand-up in a room full of cool, smart women, who are all thinky and postmodern and will get me and my crazy ideas. *Plus*, I'll be raising

22. Not that I am *not* a feminist. I am. And before your lip starts curling and you get that tic thing going in the corner of your eye, *so are you*. Think not? Well, do you think you should be able to work, live, and travel wherever you like without the accompaniment or permission of a man? That you should be paid the same amount of money as a guy for doing the same job? That you should be able to bitch-slap your guy friends when you beat them at air hockey? Then you are a feminist. Pure and simple. Stop fearing the f-word. I do think we've reached the point where we don't need to proclaim it baldly

money for little girls all over the world, and will fall asleep feeling all smug and self-satisfied. Oh, the blessing that is comedy! Oh frabjous day!"

So, I go to the show, and it's fun enough. I get to meet all the important ladies involved with the show. I know they're important because they're wearing suits. They're wearing suits, at night, in a comedy club, so people will know they're important. After hours and out of school, suits are only worn by important people. Not *very* important people, because very important people don't need to wear a suit. They ooze importance, and have toadies and lackeys genuflecting at every turn, so a suit would just be overkill. But mildly important people must wear the suit to indicate they are important, that they have given money, or sat on a board, or instructed someone in how to do things, or will be giving a speech. The suit is the thing that differentiates them from the rest of us normal, out-in-a-club-at-night-wearing-normal-old-casual-clothes people. And being from *Ms.*, they were in a lot of wonderfully tweedy pantsuits, and big blazers, and other vestments

) SWERVE (

---

from the front of our cheaply silkscreened T-shirts, jiggling braless down Main Street. Our actions, aspirations, and accomplishments should speak for themselves. Not that we've reached wage equality by any means, but we are blingin' up a storm. Women who still do feel the need to proclaim it baldly seem to be, I have found, judgmental, elitist, hypocritical pains in the asses. Which is why the rest of us don't want to claim them.

Oh, FYI, most guys are feminists too. Don't tell *them* that, though.

of midlevel power. We took a bunch of pictures together, and I got to meet Gloria Steinem, who seems like a lovely person, and has done a lot for women's rights, and also for the cause of bulky turtlenecks and giant eyeglass frames, and so deserves my respect, suit or no.

So I figure this is a group of women, and I'm a woman, and what could be better, and I'll get up there and be my edgy, anti-establishment little self, and it'll all be great. And it was, for a while. I was telling the jokes, they were laughing, and all was as it should be with the world. I could almost hear the cha-ching clink of money being put into the hands of whatever people were going to benefit from this evening of ribaldry. It was great.

Then I did a joke—and it's important to note here that they had been completely with me up to that point—that brought everything to an ass-scrubbing halt. It's also important to note that my act is not one of these girly-girl acts where I spend forty-five minutes beating up on guys, saying how they suck, and don't understand women, and leave the toilet seat up, and steal the remote, and *Whoo, aren't televised sports events boring?* And *He couldn't find my g-spot with a map and a sherpa,* and *Guys are so dumb you could hide their car keys just by moving them to the left,* and *Why don't guys understand that we'd rather be shopping instead of being ground away on by some sweaty ball of body hair!* I tend to skewer everyone pretty equally, guys and girls, because I don't see comedy as some gender war, boys against the girls, with us lined up facing each other across a battlefield, lobbing rubber chickens and cheeky one-liners across the abyss, trying desperately to hit someone in the face with a cream pie. I believe everyone should laugh at a comedy show, not just the people in the audience whose naughty bits match those of the person on stage.

So I did this bit, and it's a bit about drinking, and I won't bore you with it here, because it requires a lot of physical comedy to make it sail, and you're reading right now and so the best I could do would be some little drawn figures or something, and I can't draw for shit. Suffice it to say that the bit is about drinking too much, and then throwing up uncontrollably, and there's a line in the bit where I joke about a bulimic giving a drunk advice about throwing up, the premise being, of course, that the bulimic is an expert at the regurgitory arts. It's a quick line, a throwaway, really, but a good one. This line in this bit gets a laugh every time I do it. It is a fail-safe line. Boys, girls, old ladies, the infirm, security guards, waitresses, my mom—everybody laughs at this joke.

Except, it turns out, for grouchy feminists in scratchy wool suits. Who thought my joke was insensitive. And *hissed* me. *Hissed me!*

I could have been mad, but I wasn't. I was mostly confused. So confused that I came up short and had to think about it for a minute, while still on stage, in the middle of the bit. What had happened? Was my fly down? Had I spit in someone's eye? Had they secretly replaced my good, smart, cool audience with another, simple-minded, comedy-impaired audience? One with a slow air leak?

So I was thinking and thinking (while the audience waited), and then I got a little mad. Just a little. I don't normally get mad on stage, because no one paid to see a rage performance. They paid to see a comedy performance. If they wanted to watch rage on parade they could turn on CNN and watch Donald Rumsfeld sputter at the White House press corps for an hour or two. But they had come to see me do comedy. And I couldn't understand for the life of me why I wasn't entitled to make a joke about bulimia. Me, being a girl, a girl who has thrown up before (because really, who hasn't?) and a girl who has thrown up from drinking too much before (again, really, who hasn't?) and a girl who has, once or twice or three times, after a particularly bad set of personal choices involving food, choices driven by emotional crisis of some kind or another, and only in college, before I was old enough to fully understand how stupid such a thing really was, and at a time when I felt bulletproof and invincible, able to manipulate and abuse my body repeatedly and mercilessly, without concern for repercussion or future health . . . thrown up on purpose.

I began to get really mad, because then I started to feel as if maybe this audience, these guardians of the female, these self-proclaimed arbiters of the appropriate, maybe felt as if they *owned* bulimia, like no one else was entitled to discuss it or deconstruct it outside of their prescribed set of circumstances, like maybe in a tearful tell-all keynote speech at a conference in a hotel ballroom in Boston over watery coffee and Xeroxed handouts, or in a somber tell-all confessional in a magazine (but not too hip a magazine, certainly not one in which one might apply any kind of humor to the situation—*Ms.*, or maybe *Harper's*), or in a gut-wrenching tell-all memoir like Marya Hornbacher's *Wasted* (which, by the way, kicks ass—but there is not one moment of humor, not even the wry or ironic kind). Apparently, there was only room for one kind of story, and one kind of voice in their little stuck-in-the-seventies diorama, one where all guys are sexual predators, strip clubs are picketed, women never call each other "girl," and we can not joke about anything even mildly gender-sensitive, no matter whether we have firsthand experience with that gender-sensitive thing or not (which would completely invalidate such incredibly affecting works as Lori Gottlieb's *Stick Figure*, which is the most hilarious memoir I've ever read. It also happens to be about anorexia, but that doesn't make it any less funny).

Well, now I was really grouchy. I had been standing there on stage, thinking and grouchening, thinking and grouchening, probably not as long as it felt like to me, but long enough for crickets to start chirping and tumbleweed to start blowing across the stage, and for a couple of the more polite young ladies to begin clearing their throats. At this point, I was so pissed I felt I had to say something about the hissing. I guess I could have gone on with my act as if nothing had happened, but that seemed a bit disingenuous. I mean, we all heard the hissing, didn't we? Everybody heard the hissing. I'm sure some people would have acted as if they hadn't, but after all, it was a comedy club, not the Colosseum. Everyone heard the hissing. If I went on without addressing the hissing, then everyone would wonder, "Is she deaf? Did she not hear the hissing? Is she so unbelievably self-involved that she doesn't react when people express their extreme displeasure by making high-pitched sounds through pursed lips? What an egotist!"

It became abundantly clear there was no way I could go into the next bit without it seeming as if there was a glitch in the Matrix, so I decided to say something about it. And I did, a rant that effectively ended the "comedy" portion of my comedy act. Essentially, what I sputtered in a veiny, red-eyed rage is this: The truth is, that for all of their old-school feminist establishment snobbery, for all their hissing and pursing of lips, it wasn't like they were all there in hemp muumuus and vintage Birkenstocks, braiding their leg and armpit hair between acts. They were wearing makeup, and pantyhose, and high heels, and hairspray, and a variety of makeup products of dubious provenance. (Honestly? Some needn't have bothered.) They weren't rejecting Western norms of beauty or making a personal statement against the impossible physical standards held forth by The American Media. They were just as polished and shined and buffed and pressed and coiffed as the next woman. And if the old mathematical equation stands, that the modern beauty machine, with its unattainable standards of thinness and perfection, flawlessness and decoration, is to blame for young girls abusing themselves to within inches of their lives, then anyone who feels self-righteous enough to appoint themselves arbiter of What's Funny and Not Funny When It Comes to Women and Eating Disorders should be wearing a burlap bag, sporting a buzzcut, and walking barefoot.

Let me say here, in the clearest terms possible, that I do not think that anorexia and bulimia are funny, or that women who are truly suffering from these heartbreaking and deadly diseases should be mocked. I have had people I love, people very close to me, come very near death as a result of their EDs. Let me state again, for the record, and especially for the people who are going to take what I've said in this chapter completely out of context and make me out to be some kind of weightist bigot, that *I do not think bulimia is funny*. But, I do think that irony, applied correctly, can be a very effective form of social criticism in almost any situation (see aforementioned *Stick Figure*). And that, I humbly advance, is what I was trying to do with my teensy, tinsy little joke about the girl being counseled on barf techniques in the nightclub bathroom.

Clearly, irony is a lost art. Lost on the *Ms.* Foundation, anyway.

*   *   *

Women, on the whole, have had to lose their sense of humor in order to make personal and professional advances. To be taken more seriously, we've had to be more serious. But I also feel that leaves us unable to laugh at ourselves, to let some of the steam out of the sociocultural zeppelin. Maybe if we saw a lot of these cultural pressures, to be thin, be perfect, be fabulous, as ironic, *as a joke*, we wouldn't take them to heart so truly, be pierced by them so deeply. We could enjoy them for what they are—ideas, fashion, postmodern art—instead of fulfillment manuals, how-to books for happiness. Being able to laugh, at things that are threatening, at people that are threatening, at yourself, gives you such freedom. It takes away that "If I don't get this job, or kiss this person, or cover up my boob before the whole company picnic sees it, I'm going to die" feeling. You laugh, you get a different job, a better smoocher comes along, you've got great boobs and now everyone knows it. Life is good.

I think there are lots of things that are off-limits when it comes to humor, especially humor about women, but I think there are plenty that aren't. And I don't think you should be some kind of idiot hyena, tittering away like a drunken Hilton sister right before your car swerves off the road into a tree.

I'm just saying, jeez, lighten up a bit.

And lay off the hissing. It's rude.

Boone's Farm & Spanish Fly

There's a beer ad I remember seeing once, one of those arty black-and-white photographs where they try to trick you into thinking, for a moment or two, that maybe it's not an ad, but just a great photo of really sexy people, admirable people, cool people, people you'd like to be, and they just *happen* to be drinking lite beer.[23] The fact that they're drinking lite beer doesn't make them cool—everyone knows that lite beer is quite possibly the lamest beverage in the entire world, and cannot even be drunk in an ironic way, no matter how you try. You can drink hot tea, or Cold Duck, or Mad Dog 20/20, or even Boone's Farm Strawberry Cooler

23. I know that this is not *Webster's* preferred spelling of the word *light*, but it's the only spelling that truly communicates how awful *lite* beer is. Bleah.

ironically; all are so awfully uncool that drinking them becomes kind of funny and wry, and thus very cool. Hell, you could even drink water, which would make you seem disciplined and mysterious and make people wonder about you: are you training for an ironman triathlon, did you just get your ninety-days-sober chip, do you have to get up early for a deep-sea fishing expedition the next day, are you recovering from a life-threatening operation? The possibilities for intrigue are endless. But you cannot, no matter how you try, make an Amstel Light cool. And that's okay. You're a girl, and you're at a bar, and you don't want to ingest twelve hundred calories in the form of fermented barley. That's fine. Just know that it's a lame, TGI-Friday's-at-the-mall-on-a-Saturday-night kind of drink, and let it go. Most guys don't care what you drink anyway, as long as it has some alcoholic content of *some* kind.

But beer companies keep trying to come up with some kind of product positioning that will make lite beer seem cool, seem sexy, seem like what all the kids are drinking nowadays, when the only people drinking it are sorority girls, guys trying to drop a few "lbs," and your auntie, who drinks a lite beer and then chases it with a double-decker barbecue and onion ring cheeseburger at the family's annual Fourth of July barbecue, and doesn't seem to see the futility in any of it.

So this advertisement, in its effort to be cool, had a black-and-white photo of some incredibly gorgeous, half-naked people, which is pretty standard for beer ads,[24] and had some kind of slogan in it that wasn't about beer at all, but about something else. The wording was something along the lines of "confidence is the strongest aphrodisiac." Of course, this slogan applied not even a smidge to the photo, which was of a very hot, very cut guy with no shirt on, surrounded by very hot, very cut girls in bathing suits. Of *course* he was confident. He had twelve-pack abs, was surrounded by a pack of flesh-hungry bikini wolves having his portrait taken by Annie Leibowitz, and had all the beer he could drink. He was in dude heaven.

The intended implication, I suppose, is that if you are confident, you won't need beer to attract the other sex, because your magnetism and scintillating personality will do that for you. You will ooze poise and self-assurance like a liquid cloud of Spanish fly, and the opposite sex will flock to you, a bucket of ice-cold brewskis in tow. A more literal interpretation of the ad might be that being confident will make you look like the hot-cut beer guy and will make roving packs of bikini wolves converge on you in a smooch-thirsty frenzy. An even more simple-minded take-away would be that beer makes you confident, so go out

24. Just once I'd like to see a beer ad that showed a cross-section of the people who truly drink a majority of the beer in this country—dumpy, sallow, thirtysomething guys with beer guts and trailing, greasy mullets, watching NASCAR from a hand-me-down fold-out couch in their parents' basement, having just called in sick to their job at Meineke. Now that's sexy.

and get fucked up enough to muster up the courage to talk to some girls who will hopefully also be fucked up enough to be duped into sleeping with you. I have a suspicious feeling this is the bottom line most people glean from the ad.

I actually have no problem with the sentiment expressed by the evil genius copywriters behind this ad. I do think that confidence is the single sexiest quality a person can exude. It trumps all else: looks, money, big fake boobs, speedy European coupe, sparkling white teeth. Someone who is confident is irresistible, no matter their peculiarities, shortcomings, and flaws. Just look at all the wimpy-dumpy guys with absolutely gorgeous, fantastic, sensational women. I'm sure some of those guys have some kind of bedroom trickery that has put these women under a spell of nookie possession, but most of them are just guys that are comfortable in their own skin: funny, self-aware, disarmingly vulnerable, and enjoying life rather than enduring it. The same is true of women: there are these girls who always seem to be surrounded by guys, even though they might not be gorgeous in the lite beer sense of the word, but they are funny, and goofy, and self-effacing, and undaunted, and revel in their own specific beauty, in what makes them special, what is unique and sexy about them and them alone. Confidence, true comfort with and joy in who they are, makes them radiant. These women are magnets for men. I have heard so many guys say that they dated a drop-dead beautiful girl, one of those girls who flips her hair and has long nails she *didn't* buy in a Laotian salon, and who can wear hot pants and actually look cute rather than desperate and needy, who's perfect in all those annoying ways that make you want to put your fist through a plate-glass window. And these guys were all excited, and thought they had hit the mother lode, actually had little visualizations of them finding the pot of gold at the end of the rainbow, and inside was this girl, all long fingernails and belly-button rings, and then they spend some time with her, and they can't dump her fast enough, because she was self-absorbed, prissy, uninformed, uninteresting, a jerk.

Perfect people often are jerks, because it takes a lot of work to be perfect. Being obsessed with your looks, obsessed with perfection, takes up time that could be better spent reading, or traveling, or learning to skateboard, or ice climbing, or engaging in an all-night snaps tournament[25] (for the world championship title!) with your friends. Being perfect means looking down on everyone else who is imperfect, it means putting yourself on a pedestal, which generally keeps you from living a real, authentic life. The fact is, everybody is imperfect. Everybody is uncool. Everybody burps, and poops, and cries, and gets food caught in their teeth, and says dumb things around people they're trying to impress, and stumbles and falls in front of very important people, and had that moment in

25. "Yo' mama's cooking is so nasty . . ." Discuss amongst yourselves.

high school, or college, or a month ago, when they went up to someone that they had really intense feelings for, and proceeded to melt down like a pat of butter in a microwave in front of god and a crowd of people that included a couple of exboyfriends and their boss.

In reality, we're all lite beer drinkers. Get over it.

The War of Art

or

Aiken versus Studdard
in the World Series of Love

I am very grateful to the Japanese.

I have a lot to thank them for. Sushi is one of my favorite foods. I love Japanese art. I am obsessed with *animé*—Japanese action cartoons—even though everyone's eyeballs and breasts are drawn on roughly the same ridiculously outsized scale. (How do these women fight with all that rack in the way?) Most of my life has been dominated entirely by Japanese culture, including my four-year love affair with Hello Kitty, the summer I ate nothing but Cup O' Noodles (but only the one with the tiny dried shrimp and the "egg"), my collection of erasers that smelled like cherry, bubble gum, and "pink" (they consider this a flavor, apparently), my mom's inexplicable run of collecting Keroppi lunchboxes,[26]

26. A frog-like member of the Hello Kitty family. Where does he live, you ask? In a big house on the edge of Donut Pond. According to Sanrio.com, a website that is definitely *not* bookmarked in my browser.

my complete obsession with the show *Iron Chef*, and every piece of technological equipment in my living room. The Japanese have a hold on me. I'm not gonna lie.

But nothing that has come before compares to karaoke.

Karaoke is the great equalizer.

Karaoke is king.

If you have not tried karaoke, you have not lived. It is, at its most pure, the rawest and most exposing experience there is. People's souls are bared up there on that two-by-four plywood stage. People weep. I have seen friendships repaired (the best way to do this is a three-woman choreographed performance of Vanity 6's "Sex Shooter"), love affairs kindled (Nine Inch Nails' "Closer"), silent pleas and confessions made (Sugar Hill Gang's "Rapper's Delight," because we have all, at some point, been to a friend's house and the food just ain't no good). Every fantasy, every unfulfilled desire, every tearful expression of emotion can be channeled through an all-bar rendition of either Def Leppard's "Photograph" or Fiona Apple's "Criminal." Yes, the traditionalists go for Sinatra or Diamond or Blue Oyster Cult, but it's the adventuresome that really bare their hearts. The entire spectrum of human emotion—it's all there, in the stained, frayed pages of that big, slightly sticky binder.

When it comes to doing karaoke, there are two kinds of people. There are the people for whom this night out, this Wednesday evening or Saturday afternoon, is the single ray of light in their otherwise turbid life. These are the people who come to karaoke in teams, who know all the regulars, who point at the DJ, and wink "the usual." I have seen these people arrive in costume, in capes they've sewn themselves, in tearaway pants, in attack formation, just *itching* to get up there and bust out the choreography they worked out over the weekend to "Bootylicious."[27] They work the crowd, gyrate on tables, have microphone tricks involving their feet and the cord. These people love the limelight so much they could eat it with a knife and fork. They are always ready with a finger point or a hip snap or a *jazz hands!* when the occasion calls. I like to call them the Clay Aikens. While I may share their love of the art form, I am not one of these people. Mainly because I cannot sew.

The other kind of karaoke person is the one that insists they are there because a friend insisted, that this is the most ridiculous, outrageous, embarrassing thing in the world, that doing karaoke in front of a bunch of strangers in a bar where the wine comes in screwtop mini-bottles is a fate worse than death. They roll their eyes, guffaw out loud, they point, and smirk, and titter into their hands, and are generally all kinds of cool. That, or they are falsely shy, spending twenty minutes covering their faces and turning red and generally falsifying a state of extreme mortification. And when their friends push them to go up, they protest, "Oh no, I couldn't, I've never, I'm an aw-

27. I don't think you're ready for this jelly.

ful singer, I wouldn't know what to do, I have a canker sore, I'm Amish, I'm allergic to microphones." They're up there, mike in hand, all protestations and bashfulness, and the music goes on, all of a sudden they're Gloria freaking Gaynor, all disco spins and quavering vibrato. These people, while slightly annoying, are the most fun, mostly because of the truckload of ridicule you are able to dump on them immediately after they exit the stage. I like to call these people the Ruben Studdards, because of their overweening (im)modesty. While I often feel bashful myself in karaoke settings (it's only *proper*, after all) I will not deny the fact that I can't wait to follow the bouncing ball.

The same can be said of dating. When it comes to meeting guys, there are two kinds of girls. There are the ones who come into a club all cleavage and sequins, legs and thighs, looking for all the world like a walking bucket of chicken. These are blunt-force players, and their style is akin to throwing a big bucket of nice, juicy chum into shark-infested waters. If you spread it around enough, *some* toothsome creature is bound to swim up. Contrary to popular belief, showing your boobs to whatever boob will take a gander, while effective, is not in any way efficient. You are bound to pull the easiest, and sadly, sleaziest (hey! It rhymed!) guy in the joint. There is no honor in this approach whatsoever. The bedraggled axiom "Maybe if I dress like a hooker I'll make him think of sex"[28] is a fruit-less one, guaranteed to get you the kind of guy who, if he hadn't been lucky enough to meet you and get streetwalker-type love free of charge, would be in the King Cab of his truck forking over a crumpled twenty to the real thing right now, with no attendant shame or regret whatsoever.

The other kind of girl is the one who waits around for something great to happen, who is coy and sweet and oblivious to everything (this is fake, of course), and is just jonesing for some guy to send a drink over, or ask her to dance, or kick the jukebox until it magically starts play-ing "You've Lost That Lovin' Feelin'," drop to his knees, and start crooning at the top of his lungs (whoa there, Maverick). This girl is frequently disappointed, as guys are ruled by fear of rejection, and so primarily go for afore-mentioned boobalicious hussy types, leaving our prairie fresh Girl Oblivious wondering why all she gets are the drunken, the slobbery, and the hamfisted. This is because it has taken these guys all night to work up the courage to talk to *any* girl at all, and in the interim they have been drinking (to numb the fear), producing saliva (quite drunk at this point), and balling up their hands in frustration into tiny hams (goes along with the screwing up of the courage).

28. Everything makes guys think of sex. Rain-soaked two-by-fours make guys think of sex. Lay off it.

As a result, this girl does not have her pick of the litter, but rather is left with the actual litter, the detritus of the evening, and goes home thinking that all guys are drunken, rude, spitty, or have giant meat clubs for hands.

In my humble opinion, the optimal strategy lies somewhere in the middle. Granted, both approaches have worked countless times; in karaoke the unctuously humble Studdards provide much needed relief from the grandstanding Aikens, who, if left to their own devices, would have confetti and pyrotechnics and a sixty-member backup dance troupe brought into the seventeen-seat karaoke dive. Conversely, the openly demonstrative Aikens are a palate cleanser for the Studdards, whose faux modesty is disingenuous. C'mon, just admit you want the microphone more than life itself and stop being such a priss about it!

If you could craft an approach that used the best elements of both—the showmanship of the Aiken with the understated approach of the Studdard—you'd have an approach that would kill, every single night.

A date with a really old Chinese guy

Like everyone else in the entire world who has wanted to feel cool and hyperintellectual, I have read Sun Tzu's *The Art of War*.

Let me rephrase that. I read *part* of *The Art of War*. The first part. I tried to read the whole thing, really I did. I struggled with it, the arcane language, the obscure references (you can't get more obscure than twenty-five-hundred-year-old Chinese battle manuscripts) the multiple translations by other arcane, obscure Chinese guys—I really made the effort. I wanted it. Just not bad enough. Every night, when I'd settle in to gingerly digest another page of admonitions about how many ounces of silver per day my war effort would cost, or what provisions to lay in for a long winter siege of a northern city, something more urgent would come up. The buzzer on my dryer would go off, or there would be a *Making the Band* marathon on, and I would have to reluctantly set the book down and tend to more pressing issues. After a while, I lost track of the draught oxen and the mail-clad soldiers and whether, if forced to fight in a salt marsh, you should have water and grass near you, or get your back to a clump of trees. I also couldn't remember why I felt I needed to read this book in the first place, plopped it down on the side table, and went back to watching a farting dog fly around the set of *Jimmy Kimmel Live*. *I'll go back to reading magazines,* I giggled to myself. *More pictures, easier to carry, free perfume. Magazines are better,* I smiled as I dozed off. *Magazines and flying, farting doggies. Much, much better.*

I regret it now, because two hundred and seventeen magazine articles later, I don't feel one iota smarter; to the contrary, I think my run of reading *Men's Health* may have been rather self-destructive (I spent a week eating Dinty

Moore Beef Stew because the magazine said it was a good source of protein; I also spent that week being followed by a pack of wild dogs); and I think that, aside from the salt marsh and draught oxen thing, there is a lot to be gleaned from the old Chinese guy when it comes to dealing with the opposite sex. Am I the first person to make this intriguing but rickety comparison? I think not. Am I the first to commit it to the page in a book that also includes several fine curse words? I am proud to say I believe so.

So you're going out on a Saturday night, and for the last few weeks (or months, or years—come on, we're friends here, no need to front) you've been on a dry spell so arid you're starting to hack up sand. You need a new stratagem, a fresh approach to the age-old dilemma of "How the hell am I gonna get me some sweet, sweet lovin' tonight?" Well, let's see what Sun Tzu, a man who lived three thousand years ago, lived on rice porridge, led legions of men into battle, and probably never knew the tender touch of a woman, had to say about it.

 Sun Tzu said: Hold out baits to entice the enemy. Feign disorder, and crush him.

Of course, you don't want to crush him in the literal sense of the word. That would be cruel and *entirely* counterproductive. Instead, this is about taking a subtle, strategic approach to hooking up. What you want is to go for oblique enticement, not full frontal assault, and certainly not looking like the ninety-nine other tarts that have squeezed themselves into last year's Rampage line and are teetering around like a walking sausage parade. If all you want is sex, by all means, rack it up. Wear those pants that give you the butt cleavage.[29] Display your thong to whomever will ogle. But if you want quality, my dear, you need to put the girls away. They could probably use a rest anyway. You need to *know* you're the best thing in the room on two wheels, and act accordingly. And that means not making constant Geoffrey Holder eyes at a guy all night while squeezing your boobs between your elbows.

 Sun Tzu said: Let your plans be dark and impenetrable as night, and when you move, fall like a thunderbolt.

Take it easy. Be cool. Have a good time with your friends. Don't obsess the whole night about how to clamp down on your intended love machine. You'll have a lot more fun if you're not hell-bent on staring someone down with your voodoo X-ray vision, and he won't think you're trying to hypnotize him and steal his car keys. Enjoy yourself, laugh, have a good time. You'll seem like the coolest, most fun girl in the bar (or beach party, or dental hygienist mixer), and you will be. You seem to be having a good

29. No matter what the magazines tell you, this is not cleavage. It is plumber's butt, pure and simple. Vertically creeping ass is a bad thing; always has been, always will be.

time (which you are) and yet, strategically, you leave just enough of an opening so that if he's interested, he'll make his move. Once he hits the opening, you can make your own move, and he won't know what hit him. And if for some reason he's a blockhead, and never connects, it won't seem as if you were waiting for him to. Either way, your night will be salvaged.

> *Sun Tzu said: The control of a large force is the same principle as the control of a few men: it is merely a question of dividing up their numbers . . . Regard your soldiers as your children and they will follow you into the deepest valleys; look upon them as your own beloved sons and they will stand by you even unto death.*

While much of my ranting so far has been about being your own woman, I don't advocate you go it alone, like some freakish female James Bond, traveling the world in search of exotic trim, always the center of the baccarat table and yet always in bitter solitude. Moving with a wingwoman or three is always the best attack formation. The wingwoman provides several services: moral support early in the evening, and physical support in the wee hours; a second, somewhat objective eye to keep you from making out like a nineteenth-century Irish strumpet with the drunk guy with the forehead tattoo who you think, if you squint, *"kind* of looks like Usher combined with Slash from Guns n' Roses"; is a distraction for a guy's wingman;[30] and is a quick exit out of a bad situation should you need it (he's got a shrunken head on his keychain; loves Barbra Streisand movies; is a Libertarian). Guys have a name for female friends who perform this service. They call them *cockblockers*. What they don't seem to realize is that, in a case where your wingwoman has provided a quick get-away, they were never lined up to be blocked in the first place (if you catch my drift). The first thing a good wing-woman does, if she sees her friend is about to score, is get the hell out of the way, usually with a frantic wave of the hand and a hoarsely whispered "go for it! I checked his finger-nails! They're clean!"

Sun Tzu said: We cannot enter into alliances until we are acquainted with the designs of our neighbors.

Having a good wingwoman is important. However, you cannot just get any old chick to provide this service;

30. Usually I find beer ads insipid, but there is an excellent Budweiser commercial that illustrates this service perfectly, called "Ballad of the Wing-man." Unfortunately, it presents the guy taking the hit for his friend rather than the other way around. I cannot count the number of times I've been stuck talking to some beanball about his auto insurance underwriting job so a girl-friend of mine could run it up court into the nookie zone. Nonetheless, this is one of my favorite commercials, as evidenced by the fact that I can sing the whole thing, word for word, a capella. The fact that I have a much too highly developed relationship with my Tivo is another issue entirely.

the motives of those who have not been vetted by years of loyalty and service are unclear and may lead to tears and hair pulling later. You want to make sure you entrust a good friend with this responsibility, not just any old random girlfriend. Good friends are loyal, supportive, make you feel good about yourself, support you when you decide to enter a slam poetry contest or learn Mandarin, tell you the guy you like has a kind face when he's really homely as a rodeo clown, and never complain when you duck out on a girl's night out to go see a guy. *Girlfriends* make you feel inadequate, judge your choices, or encourage you to engage in the same self-destructive behaviors that are turning them into scrawny hollow she-ghosts that reek of gin and use sex to deal with interior fault lines that would be better handled in therapy. You want the women in your life to give you nothing but love and support. That and an occasional twenty for cab fare when you've got to get out of the place in a hurry.

 Sun Tzu said: Knowledge of the enemy's dispositions can only be obtained from other men. Be subtle! Be subtle! And use your spies for every kind of business.

This is where the wingwoman (or man) is indispensable. I actually want to make a quick case for the use of wingmen by women, and vice versa. Several of my closest friends are guys, and while it's true that going out with straight friends of the opposite sex can sometimes put some serious salt in your game ("He's *not* my boyfriend!" can get exhausting after a while), it can also be ridiculously profitable. First of all, no one is better at reading the body language and barely perceptible signals a guy is throwing out than another guy. They are excellent plants, can be sent into the camp of the enemy to retrieve information or make subtle overtures (such delicate gems as, "Isn't that chick over there insanely hot? That's *all* you, dude."), and are a second eye when yours aren't reliable. (Sometimes, female friends, out of love, won't tell you when you are barking up the wrong guy, I mean tree, but a guy friend will yell it right in your face, usually for the entire bar to hear: "That guy's a fucking tool!" Embarrassing, but valuable nonetheless.) They are also excellent ersatz lovers should the need arise to get rid of a particularly ardent (read drunk and/or stupid) suitor. The wingperson is there to make your job easier, to provide company, consultation, and an array of exit strategies should you need it. Remember to provide the same services at a later date. And whether you go for the female escort or the male, the exclamation "be subtle! be subtle!" is the most prescient double admonition I have ever read. This guy Sun Tzu was clairvoyant.

*Sun Tzu said: When the enemy is close
at hand and remains quiet, he is relying
on the natural strength of his position.
When he keeps aloof and tries to provoke
a battle, he is anxious for the other side to
advance. If his place of encampment is
easy of access, he is tendering a bait.*

Let's say you're at an arcade.[31] You've been throwing game at a hottie across the room all night long, and when you go to peep him out, he's standing right next to you dropping quarters into Time Crisis III. The game is on. Offer to go to head-to-head, 'cause you're in. Now let's say instead that you look up and he's across the room about to get into a little Dance Dance Revolution. You may have to step it up a little. But be subtle. And wait until he's stepped down off the thing—talking to someone midsong is liable to get them killed. On the other hand, if he tries to interrupt you in the middle of a 9–0 streak on TKO, let him sweat it out a bit. You've got a world title to protect.

---

31. Don't tell me I'm the only girl who thinks this is an excellent way to spend a Saturday night. The joint is just crawling with guys. Demonstrate even a rudimentary ability on a first-person shooter and you'll be the belle of the ball. Never played House of the Dead? Take it old school. I mean really, *who* can't play Ms. Pacman or Tempest? What are you, a Luddite?

Sun Tzu said: When you engage in actual fighting, if victory is long in coming, then men's weapons will grow dull and their ardor will be damped. If you lay siege to a town, you will exhaust your strength. Thus, though we have heard of stupid haste in war, cleverness has never been seen associated with long delays.

So it's late—*really* late, and the dude you've been jocking all night has turned out to be a real puss. He can't commit—he's hot and cold all night, and you can't get a read on him to save your life. One minute he's saying he wants to leave with you, the next he's having a contest in the corner with eight other guys to see who will drink the giant Long Island Iced Tea they made from everyone else's empties. Things seem at once both promising and desperate. What's more, the barkeep's just thrown on the house lights, you now look as if you've been reanimated from the dead, and he doesn't show any signs of going for the keys. What do you do?

Are you kidding me? *Go home.* Any dude that can't close a deal this good, and this ripe for the closing, is going to be a huge waste of time down the line, and by down the line I mean as soon as you get him alone. Leave with your friends, go get a late night ice-cream cone (really, it's the key to inner happiness), and thank your lucky stars you didn't have to spend the next three hours doing an entirely different brand of coaxing.

 Sun Tzu said: One may know how to conquer without being able to do it.

Let's say you've done everything right. You look gorgeous, fashionable, hot but not slutty. You've spent the night being your naturally funny, engaging, slightly klutzy (but in an endearing way) self. You've made it clear that you're feeling a certain guy, and that he could be feeling you later. But no juice. I think you know the answer. Keep partying, and cut this guy out of your plans. There is nothing more infuriating than spending an entire night trying to connect with someone, then going home alone, buzzed and slightly enraged. The increasingly desperate push to close the deal usually elicits a variety of terrifyingly bad behaviors, the most common of which is becoming obsessed with Mr. Frosty, which leads to the kind of inappropriate, self-eviscerating behavior that man-crazy girl legends are made of. If you've dropped all your bombs and he's still standing there, unscathed, playing air hockey and *not seeing you*, do not make the desperation play. The desperation play *always* ends badly. Worst case scenario, you pull something truly horrific, like falling down drunk and showing everyone your underpants, or flashing the bar (you girl gone wild!), or coming on like a Thai prostitute, guaranteeing your instant consecration into urban legend.

Best case scenario, you get what you want immediately, but don't get what you want in the long run (when you realize you've embarrassed yourself too badly to ever really be able to kick it with this guy when both of you aren't cock-eyed drunk, and also find you have to avoid the bar, the guy, and anyone in the city who has access to the newspaper, the Internet, or three stalls in the bar's men's bathroom).

 Sun Tzu said: What the ancients called a clever fighter is one who not only wins, but excels in winning with ease.[32]

Meeting people is hard, but trying to connect with someone shouldn't feel like the finale of every Benny Hill episode. You don't have to be a female Shaft, dispensing cool one-liners and platform-shoe ass kickings with equal ease, but if getting to a guy requires a lot of subterfuge, conniving, machinations, or sleight of hand (like if you have to climb in windows, pop up from behind things, feign mortal illness, or cry) you might want to rethink your

32. Who *are* these ancients? Sun Tzu lived five hundred years *before* Christ. *He's ancient.* I can't imagine what ancients he's talking about. Assyrians? Sumerians? Maybe his idea of ancient is a few hundred years or so—back then they may not have had the same depth perception we have now when it comes to history, seeing as they didn't have medicine or refrigerators and had to poop into a hole in the ground and routinely died of things like colds and toothaches. Wait, I just looked it up on the Internet and Chinese civilization is like five thousand years old, and some archaeologists believe it may even be as much as ten. That is pretty damned ancient. Man, those Chinese had it together. Although that's a long time to be civilized without inventing the toilet.

approach. Unless he's a *really* incredible guy (You must *know* this in some way first! Do not just assume because he's got eyes like saucers and lips like a girl that he's worth splaying yourself out over!), then all bets are off. But even then, remember, if you begin a relationship with a guy based on manipulation, you're going to have to maintain the deception throughout your time together, which is exhausting, and as almost every episode of every eighties sitcom proves, will end badly, with either your wig falling off in public, your French accent coming in and out during an important dinner party, or you almost having sex with a guy old enough to be your father. Take it easy. I don't want to coin a dogeared phrase from The Electric Company, but you made me do it: be yourself.

Sun Tzu said: It is a military axiom not to advance uphill against the enemy, nor to oppose him when he comes downhill. Do not pursue an enemy who simulates flight; do not attack soldiers whose temper is keen. Do not swallow bait offered by the enemy. Do not interfere with an army that is returning home. When you surround an army, leave an outlet free. Do not press a desperate foe too hard.

Do not chase a guy down. It's okay to step into his territory but do not spend all your time "coincidentally" materializing two millimeters from his elbow when he least expects it. You will not seem fabulous and mysterious; you will seem creepy and nefarious. If he approaches you, great, be open, but don't exhale as if you've been on a two-week hunger strike and your thick-crust double pepperoni pizza just arrived. If a guy looks like he's going to leave, but doesn't invite you along, do not wildly blurt out that you "don't have anything to do and are just dying to eat chicken and watch porn with a group of strange guys." Let him know it'd be cool if he called you sometime. Glomming on lets him know it'd be cool if you guys had six-and-a-half minutes of furtive sex in the back of his Geo Metro. If he and his friends are leaving, let him know you'd like *him* to stay, but if he says he can't, say good-bye, especially if the rest of his crew looks like they want to eat you for lunch (and I don't mean that in the sexy figurative way). If he *wants* to stay, he'll blow them all off. Guys'll blow off their friends for an extra flauta at a taco stand—rely on his natural capacity for self-interest. If you are trying to get a guy to leave with you, be subtle about it. Do not press him up into a corner like a horny Burgess Meredith and try to pull his mouthguard out with your tongue. This will not get you what you want. Unless what you want is to weird him out, demonstrate your poor decision making skills, and become the most "popular" girl in that bar for all time. "Popular" meaning slutty.[33]

---

33. What's the rule? Respect yourself.

This is not about playing games and seeming like you don't care. This is about guys' generally fragile margin of comfort with women and their tendency to implode into dust like an Amaretto cookie when they feel unduly pressed, and your need to maintain a modicum of coolness so you have somewhere safe to retreat to if things start to go south. Be very clear: you cannot pull back from a full frontal assault—once you bring the pain, the artillery's there on the battlefield for everyone to see. There's nothing like emptying both chambers only to get dismissed without ceremony by a guy who you later realize would never have passed muster if you hadn't had that fifth Cuba Libre. Guys know this, which is why they play it so close to the vest. Which is why you will never find out that a guy you were incredibly hot for also liked you back until months after you've already started dating someone else and the proverbial ship has sailed: you've had sex with the new guy many times, made him your famous oven-baked French toast casserole, promised to meet his family. The ship is you, if you're not following my metaphor.

Sun Tzu said: There are five dangerous faults which may affect a general:

1. *Recklessness, which leads to destruction;*
2. *Cowardice, which leads to capture;*
3. *A hasty temper, which can be provoked by insults;*
4. *A delicacy of honor, which is sensitive to shame;*
5. *Over-solicitude for his men, which exposes him to worry and trouble.*

I think this is pretty self-explanatory. We've all watched other women blow a good thing by cracking up in one way or another when, if they had just held on a little longer, they'd have been leaving the bar triumphantly, deer carcass strapped firmly to their wrist. That being said, a little modern translation:

1. **Recklessness,** which leads you to make out madly with a guy whom, upon reflection (and a little tongue exploration), you realize doesn't have an entire set of teeth and came out tonight on the bus;

2. **Cowardice,** which keeps you from talking to a guy who appears, for all intents and purposes, to be the answer to your every life's question, or at the very least like he'd look great naked;

3. **A hasty temper,** which leads you to get annoyed rather than laugh when a guy hits you with a little good-natured ribbing, revealing that you are a cold, cold fish of a woman with a black heart and absolutely no sense of humor;[34]

4. **A delicacy of honor** which is sensitive to shame, which leads you to be haughty and remote when Justin Timberlake's doppelganger is trying to get you to dance (depending on what city you're in, it might actually *be* Justin Timberlake) thus losing out on the biggest night of your life, and depriving your friends and family of years and years of colorful, detailed, incredibly exaggerated storytelling;

5. **Over-solicitude,** which leads to indiscriminate behavior, such as working your way down an entire line of guys at a bar until you find one who doesn't realize he's sloppy seconds. Or fifths. Or twenty-fifths (not that you're particularly sloppy, but no one likes knowing they didn't make the top five). Have some pride, woman!

34. On the other hand, if he makes disparaging comments about your hair, breasts, face, friends or the San Francisco 49ers, skedaddle. If the guy's got that kind of disrespectful hubris now, think of how bad he'll be after you've done a little of the naughty ab-crunching.

Sun Tzu said: Hence to fight and conquer in all your battles is not supreme excellence; supreme excellence consists in breaking the enemy's resistance without fighting.

Do not obsess, panic, try to control, manipulate, coerce, cajole, guilt, embarrass, wheedle, or whore a guy into bed with you.

 Aisha said: Be cool. Have fun. Good things will come.[35]

35. I just noticed this bears a striking resemblance to a Pepsi slogan. I apologize. My aphorisms aren't usually this treacly.

The Boy Scout Motto: Be Prepared

What I am about to say may seem radical to you. If you feel faint, or weak of heart, or if you were recently dumped unceremoniously by a good-for-naught jackass whose idea of romance was to pester you constantly for a threesome with your teenaged cousin, take a breather. This is not for the pudding-willed.

Guys and girls can be friends. Good, platonic (that means *no sex*) friends.

I know I am flouting the rules that make up the very fiber of the universe we live in. I know that these words throw sand in the face of creation and all who occupy it. But it's true. If I am known for nothing else, let me be known for telling the truth. And having a good sense of humor.

And making a mean margarita.

I know this is true, because I have one. I have several good ones, actually, and one best one. That's right, my best friend is a boy.[36] Look away, hiss in disgust, cast your eyes downwards in shame, call me a turncoat, I care not. My best friend is a boy, and I don't care who knows it! He is a boy I have known for many years to be loving, compassionate, giving, thoughtful, and caring. He's a sweet guy, plus he can do a mean shot and he laughs at my jokes, which is an instant A-plus in my book.[37]

This has many benefits. All of the mysteries of the male universe are made clear to me, including why a game show with the same four contestants sputtering at each other about obscure sports points, in which the winner doesn't win any money or stuff or even a trip to Florida, can possibly be interesting every single day.[38] He is also a good resource for questions about foot fungus, obscure high-proof alcohols, why guys are obsessed with boobs,

36. This is not counting my beloved husband, who is my number one best friend, but because I am making a point about platonic friendship, does not qualify under these particular criteria. When I use the term *best friend* I am using it much in the way a girl would use it if she was referring to a female best friend, and thus, if she mentioned her best friend, you would assume it was a girl and not her spouse (unless she was a lesbian, and then all bets are off, as she is surrounded by a world of potential too great and wonderful to comprehend). But because my best friend is male, I have to distinguish him from my husband, who is also my best friend, who is also male. I could call him my "best male platonic friend," but then I would sound like a pompous ass.

37. The book that I keep that has everybody's grades in it. Yours are in there, too. There'll be a test at the end of this.

38. *Around the Horn* on ESPN. Sadly, in trying to expose this show for the mealy-centered fraud that it is, I got hooked. Get 'em Woody! Bring the pain, Holley! In yo' face, Kellerman!

and early Eric B. and Rakim B-sides. And he's funny, too. Not as funny as me, but what can you do?

One of the things I like best about my boy friend is that he tells me stories. Lots of awful, dirty, boys' ears only stories. He is not proper, or prim, or delicate around me. We are friends, and as such, I am a buddy first, and a girl second. Because of this, I get the skinny. The down low. Dirt-o-rama. I love this, because guys are never real around girls. Either they are trying to sleep with you, impress you, or gross you out. It is only when you are true friends with guys that you get the unvarnished version. And that is what I get from him. It is most excellent.

I cannot relate all these stories here, because they are too numerous to mention, and because they are mine and I don't want to share. But I will tell one. It's a goody.

Before I tell this story, I want you to know that most guys are basically good. Very, very good. They are sweet, and vulnerable, and funny, and hopeful, and sensitive, except for a few waterheaded numbskulls that should be thrown in the ocean and picked apart by giant barracuda (you know who you are). But the rest of them are great. Unless we're talking about career criminals or the insane, most guys are entirely capable of falling in love. It isn't as if there's one kind of guy who's a dog, and another who spends his life waiting to fall on a bended knee, platinum five-karat Tiffany solitaire at the ready. The mistake we make is not realizing that guys have the capacity for *both* behaviors inside them—the angel and the mongrel, the dream guy and the man-whore. We make the mistake of believing that our angelic, sweet, milk-fed mama's boy couldn't possibly have a dirty mind, and that that dark-eyed, swarthy construction worker with a potty mouth and an ass like Valhalla is good only for a romp but couldn't possibly fall. The fact is, they can do both, crossing from dark side to the light depending on the situation and whether they got something to eat that morning. If we were able to recognize the disturbance in the force more regularly, we wouldn't have our bells so rung when we find out Johnny Perfect has a crushing fetish.

That being said, this story that my sweet, sweet friend told me should come as no surprise.

My friend and another friend of his were at a bar, and it was the end of the night. The place had cleared out, and it was a swordfight—a huge gaggle of guys and only two girls (I know *gaggle* probably isn't the correct plural for a group of men, but it alliterated). Through some miracle, some heaven-sent assistance, the two women approached *them*,[39] and the game was afoot.

Now, in the story, these two women are incredibly hot. Realize that in every story guys tell about picking girls up, especially those that subsequently get away, the girls are

39. I don't know these women, but I like them already.

incredibly hot, insanely sexy, "I think one of them was a swimsuit model" *fly*. So I cannot be entirely sure that these women were as high on the fineness Richter scale as they were represented to me to be. However, it makes the story that much better if they *are* hot, so I'll allow it in this case.

They go back to the girls' hotel. My friend is with a blond one, and his friend is with a brunette. They are making out on the twin beds, and they are so overwhelmed with their good fortune that they forget to be upset about the fact that they are half-naked with another straight guy in a room that doesn't provide steam therapy. They are so giddy that at one point they try to high five each other across the void between the beds; this very nearly topples them out of bed and into a naked, pantsless heap on the floor, but luckily everyone was too drunk on Hpnotiq and Red Bull to notice. They sighed a collective "phew" and got back to business. Things get hot and heavy. My friend and his buddy are so incredulous at their good fortune that they are on the verge of an aneurysm. And just when it seems like it can't possibly get any better, that he must have a secret genie, that god has chosen him personally for all the gifts and bounties this mortal coil has to offer . . . The girls start *making out with each other*.

This seems awesome. When it is told to me, I think it's awesome. I think, "Wow, this is a great freaking story. If I was a guy I would be beside myself. *Penthouse*'s 'Forum' would most certainly be interested in this ribald, piquant adventure." In all of the excitement, no one stops to wonder at the fact that these guys have been cut out of the action, rendered shivering, be-shorted, irrelevant bystanders by one girl-on-girl liplock. These things do not matter in such heady times; they are minutiae, academic, irrelevant in the face of the big picture, which is that these guys have hit paydirt, the lottery, perhaps scoring two of the coolest, most sexually adventurous girls in the entire world (at least who aren't already professionally employed in the erotic arts). I am just as swept up in the delirium of it all; I know what a night like this can mean to a guy (akin to meeting Matt Damon, or finding a pair of Jimmy Choo boots on sale for a hundred dollars); I am on the edge of my seat, breathless.

It's time to get down to business. The sun is coming up. It's either go time or breakfast time. Our boys, rubbing their hands together like Tiny Tim over a Christmas goose, go for their wallets.

No one has a condom. There are four adults in this room, and not one prophylactic between them. It's five in the morning. The hotel convenience store is closed. They're downtown. The only thing open this early are coffee shops and bakeries. Somehow, a croissant doesn't seem like it would do much good right now.

It's important to mention that this is a group of very mature, self-aware, cool people (I've never met these mystery vixens, but I infer from context). So far all has been consensual, all has been fun. No predation, no pressure, no manipulation. It's been a romp. And because these are all insanely cool people, they bring the romp to a screeching halt, because no one has a condom. That rocks so hard. Sexual adventures are all fun and games until someone recklessly throws their health and the health of others under the bus.

It quickly goes from bad to worse. The girls decide the guys are just baggage, baggage without the proper provisions, unprepared observers. They look at the guys. They look at the door. The guys look at the girls, hoping at the very least for a wee hours show. They don't get one. They are forced to leave, hats in hand, laughing hysterically to themselves at the grand fortune and irony of it all, two Little Rascals kicking an empty can of franks and beans down the street in the burgeoning light.

These guys went back to their old lives, their day jobs, their happy hours, and their friends. They did not turn into monsters. They did not troll the streets looking for another two bisexual barhoppers, hoping to duplicate the experience. They stayed nice guys, guys who loved their moms, guys who counted girls among their closest friends. A tear was shed, in the dark, for what could've been. And deep provisions were laid into wallets for the long winter ahead.

I often wonder about those girls, and that night, and the possibilities that lay before them. And then I thank my lucky stars that my best friend is a guy, and that I can hear the kind of stories that up until now, I never would have believed existed outside of low-production-value porn.

My horizons are forever widened.

The Ballad of
OshKosh B'Gosh

I once liked a boy. I liked this boy a lot. I liked this boy as if my life depended on it.

It was an awful kind of like, the kind that makes you show up at every one of his frat's parties, the kind that makes you hover near his mailbox in the student union, the kind that makes you stare at him from across the cafeteria while your soft-serve sundae with the tiny marshmallows melts into goop. The kind that makes you *call and hang up*. *That* kind of like.

This boy liked me okay, and called me sometimes, and eventually we got together, and the sex was okay. In my mind, it was stupendous, mindblowing, life-changing sex, mainly because I liked the boy so much. In reality it was just okay, sweaty, a little frustrating, and a little bit too much time spent arguing over directions, if you know what I mean. But I liked this boy, and so I quickly forgot about these things, and we started dating, and I was happy for a time, despite the fact that this boy was too much work and still couldn't seem to find his way around, despite my patient and quite detailed directions. If you know what I mean.

So after a time, this boy and I, for reasons out of our control, had to be separated. I was devastated. It had taken a lot of work to secure this boy, a lot of waiting around at mailboxes and melted sundaes, and I felt as if all my work might be for naught. So I vowed, while we were separated, that I would never look at another boy, or talk to one, that I would stay in at night, and read instead of watch *The Simpsons*, and study like a maniac (or an engineering major), and live the life of an ascetic until the boy's safe return.

And true to my vow, I did. At the time, I hadn't spent any time in a Buddhist monastery or nunnery, so I wasn't quite clear on exactly what the life of an ascetic entailed. But I did have a pair of old, baggy, and especially unflattering overalls. I decided that these would be my loincloth (metaphorically speaking) and that I would wear them constantly until the boy came back. I suppose I believed that, by not using makeup, drinking beer, or wearing any clothing that broadcast the true shape of my figure to others, I was sending a message to the universe that this boy was the boy for me, despite his flakiness and lack of directional sense, and that the universe would let him know that, and would get him back to me quickly, safely, and with a newfound knowledge of the female anatomy.

So I lived in those awful overalls. For weeks I tramped around looking like Cowboy Curtis' unkempt sister. I was morose. I was downcast. I was incredibly boring. I refused to brush my hair, and so had a giant dreadlock form that started to list dangerously to the left, threatening to give me a compressed disk, or at the very least, a crick in my neck. And I kept insisting on wearing those overalls.

As obsessively hygienic a person as I am, I simply could not keep the overalls meticulous. For one, I was too busy being Eeyore. Secondly, I had classes to attend. I couldn't spend every free minute at the laundromat. Especially since I had spent all the money I had left over from buying books on bacon pizza and chicken wings, to help assuage the emptiness I felt over the missing boy, and so had no quarters. As a result, the overalls were starting to develop a personality of their own, right about the same time that I was losing the last vestiges of mine. It didn't matter to me, though. I knew that the boy would see how much I liked him, and would come back to me, smelling like Tide detergent and Polo cologne, and a little bit like Jagermeister, and that we would live happily ever after, or at least until graduation.

The problem was that the universe paid no attention whatsoever to my overalls vigil. And the boy, being thousands of miles away, was equally oblivious. So oblivious that he didn't write or call much at all. At first, I thought maybe I wasn't committed enough to my regimen, so I slept in my overalls for a couple of days. This was when my stricken (and a little skeeved out) friends informed me that enough was enough. Well, they didn't so much tell me as show me, by picking me up and throwing me, dungarees and all, into a cold shower. After I yelled, called them many curse words, and hit one of them in the head with a bottle of conditioner, they set me straight. It didn't take long. The fact that I hadn't heard from the boy in three weeks was pretty telling. The fact that they had heard he was sleeping with the cousin of the friend of one of my roommates I took to be a bad sign as well.

At this point, I got a little angry. At the boy, yes, for cheating, and for never, ever finding his way around no matter how many times I said "to the left, *to the left*," but also at myself, for having wasted most of a semester looking like Lenny Kravitz after a bender when I could have been out, having a good time, eating soft-serve sundaes and talking to other, nicer guys with better internal compasses. I promptly burned the overalls, brushed my hair, did three shots of Jagermeister (I'm sentimental) and went out to party. I forgot about the boy, but never about what I learned lo, those not so many years ago:

1. **Get a life.** Slavish devotion is not, in any way, sexy. It is weird and will earn you the reviled moniker of psycho.[40] Which is *so* not sexy. Guys—hell, *everyone*—is attracted to a person who has an interesting and complex life. Not only that, but you'll find *yourself* more interesting. There's nothing a guy wants more than something he can't have, and there's no girl a guy wants more than one that seems like she's too busy for him. When you're personally satisfied, not only are you more sexy to him, you're more sexy to yourself. And that makes everything more sexy. So, stop being such a boy-crazy man-eater and get some hobbies. Focus on that promotion. Acquire a taste for Chilean wines. Take that bookmaking class. Skydive. For god's sake, have your own shit going on. You'll find you're a whole lot sexier when you can meaningfully participate in a conversation about U.S. foreign policy in South America, instead of contributing your old standby, "Wow, so what's up with *that?*"

2. **You time.** Take care of yourself. There are a variety of theories on why American women spend millions of dollars a year on bleaches and waxes and plucking and pruning and scraping and cutting and other pain-laced procedures far too numerous to mention here. Some

---

40. For more on this, see the footnotes in *It's Your Turn to Clean the Pole.* Man, my footnotes are referencing my other footnotes. This book is like a Gordian knot.

say we do it for guys. Some say we do it for each other. While I am a firm advocate against the surgical arts, namely pneumatic racks and Botoxed pates that make one look like Walter Cronkite in the tomb, as mentioned previously, I am a big advocate of personal up-keep. But not for guys, and not for other women, *for you*. Being sexy is about being confident, feeling good about what you've got going on, and secure in the knowledge the package looks as good as its contents. This comes from a variety of places, most of them internal, one of them knowing that the belly beard you inherited from your great aunt Tilly won't pop out of your low-rise thong and scare your new best friend off of your couch and into a cab.

3. **Don't waste time obsessing about a guy who doesn't follow directions.** Enough said.

Us versus Us

or

The Molly Ringwald Conspiracy

I have a friend, a brilliant, wonderful, beautiful friend, who is a psychologist. She is tall, curvaceous, gorgeous, with silken hair and porcelain skin. She smells nice, is hilarious, and is the kind of girl guys want to devour and girls want to hug and kiss, even girls who rarely have these impulses about other women. I idolize her. She has got to be one of the coolest, sexiest women I know.

This woman also once suffered from such cripplingly low self-esteem that she developed an eating disorder, one that almost killed her. Even through the darkest periods in her life, she was so cool and funny and fabulous that I never knew she was sick until she told me years later. When she became a psychologist, of course, she wanted to help other eating-disordered women, so she began leading eating-disorder therapy groups. One of the things she repeatedly told them was that the fashion culture was making them crazy. The unattainable images of perfection, of flawless beauty and impossible thinness, weren't real. The women in the photos in the fashion magazines were figments of the imagination, manipulated through a combination of personal suffering, contortion, airbrushing, and safety pins to look like seraphs fallen from heaven. She encouraged them to throw their fashion magazines down, cast them out as bad influences, forces of evil. *You can never look like these women*, she counseled, *because these women don't exist.*

Soon after that, her dear friend (*moi*), began appearing in the very magazines she had told others to burn ceremonially, to mark as evil. Someone she liked and respected (I think) was popping up, all boobs and lips and hair, in the camp of the enemy. *Now* what could she say? Here was someone she knew, someone very real, appearing in an unreal medium. The dynamic had ceased to be *us* versus *them*. Now it was *us* versus *us*. Which made everything *that* much more complicated.

The problem is, when it comes to the unattainable standard of perfection that is held above girls' heads, that really is the true dynamic: *us* versus *us*. It's easy to go around talking about how *they* make women feel insecure, and inferior, and less than; how *the beauty industry* has set an ideal that is impossible to attain; how it is *society* that is making women starve themselves, and go to drastic lengths to fit some idea of how they think they need to look to be beautiful. But who is the *they*? There is no shadow organization holding secret meetings to decide, over diuretic tea and dietetic biscotti, that the emaciated crack whore look is going to be all the rage for the new fall season. There *are* no meetings. There *is* no conspiracy. At least, not in the way we'd like to think of it. *We* are the conspiracy. We are the ones buying, selling, creating, generating, supporting, and perpetuating every aspect of the crazily high beauty bar we all claim to hate. We have no one to blame but ourselves.

Now, before you start lighting the corner of this book on fire (I'm amazed it hasn't been ripped to tatters by now—you have an incredible sense of self-restraint), understand that the fashion and beauty industries are, by and large, run by women. Edited, written, designed, concepted by women. Purchased almost wholly by women (and a handful of gay men). We are the engine that runs the beauty machine. We are the tiny, angry man behind the curtain in Oz.

And we can be bloodless about it. Brutal. We are the ones who call each other "thick," and "hippy," and squawk "I can't *believe* she thinks she has the body for that outfit!" when someone passes by in, say, a pencil skirt that reveals not only the wearer's thong, but what brand, size, and floral pattern. We are the ones who mutter "slut" and "tramp" and "nice boobs—lean over a little more so they can get a shot from the Hubble" when well-endowed women skitter by in unfortunately taut V-necks. We "tsk-tsk" and "uh-oh" and "mh-mh-mh-mh-mh" at women who we think are too fat, too skinny, too lumpy, too saggy, too dumpy, too perky, need makeup, have too much makeup, tease their hair, use kohl (that might be warranted), or think leggings qualify as a pant item.

The truth? This is *our* problem. Yes, there are a lot of amorphous, exterior sources and reasons why women everywhere are waging their own private interior battle against food, and clothes, and their bodies, and themselves. Yes, there is a constant, overwhelming wall of weight bearing down on girls' shoulders, telling them they should be perfect, with glossy lips, teeth like shiny peppermint Chiclets, hair that looks like it just made the leap from a pony's rump, skin like the ass of a baby bathed only in goat's milk from the leeward side of Mt. Ida, and a body like a twelve-year-old boy, with breasts like a twelve-year-old boy who's just gotten forty-thousand-dollar implants. We all feel this weight. This weight is real. I am not denying this weight is very, very real. But we could do so much to help ourselves if we would just . . . *put the weight down.*

Hah! You scoff. *Feh! Easy for you to say!* And it is, because I am typing this from the safety of my computer rather than having a face-to-face conversation with you, and so I am taking the coward's way out by tapping out these incendiary words, then running away, like that stupid bully in the third grade who hit you with a poop-covered stick, then ran down the street and hid behind her older brother.[41] I realize that. And while I don't think that we can just wish everything away by saying "I'm sorry, I don't believe in gravity. I'm going to jump out of this airplane and float awaaaaaaaaaaayyyyyy!!!!" I do believe that if we just changed how we reacted to all this stuff, if we diminished the importance it has in our day-to-day lives, we would be a lot happier. Life would be a lot sweeter. And a lot less filled with rants of "Why doesn't my ass look like Cameron Diaz's when I put on the *exact* same pair of jeans? Why?!?"

The first thing that everybody has to do, immediately, is realize that all of it is fake. It is make-believe. All of it. Fun, fantasy, dress-up, tea-party time make-believe. The images you see in fashion magazines are the product of hours of pulling and pushing and taping and pasting and pinning and smooshing and sucking in and fluffing out. This is followed by hours of posing that would make one of those human statues at Caesars in Vegas weep into his tip cup. Then comes even more modification, airbrushing and retouching and all kinds of digital trickery, the same kind of crazy voodoo geek magic that made Jar Jar Binks

41. I figure this has happened, in some form or another, to everyone at some point in their lives, some later than others. If this happened to you recently, like in the last week, my sincere apologies for rekindling the painful memories.

look like a *real* annoying platypus-donkey-Rastafarian-amphibian guy in a vest instead of a fake one.

I don't say this to crush your idealism, to snatch from you your belief that there is some kind of otherworldliness, something idealized, something aspiration-worthy, ethereal, dazzling, about these women. There is. But, in many ways, they are no more incandescent than the women you have in your own life: where you work, or go to school, or get your hair done, or buy your Chinese food; your college roommate, your sister, your best girlfriend from grade school, *you*. The ones in the magazines have just had more time and attention to pay to isolating and playing up the parts of themselves that are most beautiful. This is something anyone can do, given unlimited time, unlimited resources, and a crack team of top stylists, and there is a part of us, deep down, that knows that,[42] a part of us that is obscured by all the insecurities, and mental self-flagellation, and futile exercises in comparison.

The thing that makes us hate these images and the people in them is the same thing that makes us love them.

‿ *SWERVE* ‿

42. I think the third act of *The Breakfast Club*—specifically that scene where Molly Ringwald's snooty socialite gave Ally Sheedy's bizarre social misfit the five-minute makeover—did a lot to give a generation of young women a misguided hope that no matter how weird you were, no matter if you dressed like a mortician and wrote bad poetry about dead people and ravens and moldy corpses, and made your hair into a fake moustache by smooshing it between your nose and upper lip, and looked at everybody sidelong as if you might put a voodoo hex on them the minute you could cut off a decent lock of their hair, well, with just a little blush and lip gloss, you'd be instantaneously gorgeous and could get right back into the game again. The game being hanging out with the likes of prissy old Molly Ringwald.

They inspire us, they make us believe mere mortals can look like angels (in the case of Victoria's Secret), or at least like people so fabulously gorgeous and overwhelmingly interesting that the rest of life bores them to tears, especially walking down an elevated runway in front of hundreds of people in a dress made of diamonds and flower petals worth ten thousand dollars. This love–hate dynamic is what fuels our obsession with the beauty industry and everything else associated with it.

And we admire them because they *do* look so beautiful, so abstractly perfect, so unattainable. We enjoy idealized images. The human animal, like most animals, is addicted to beauty. So we complain about the impossibility of it all, the Grand Guignol imagery, the cheekbones and the hipbones and the collarbones and it's all so ridiculous and extreme and shocking and . . . fascinating. But it's not real.

These images are *ideas*. They are concepts, archetypes. They are not standards, or molds, or instructions. They are abstracts. Many of these women that look so extraordinary in print, that seem so impossibly inhuman, are just that: impossible. In a magazine or on a runway, they seem ethereal, floaty; in person, they are gawky, jagged, pimply, or sallow, overwhelmingly ordinary. Women whose bodies seem so equine and sinuous pony-stepping down a runway are, in person, spectacles of emaciation, sexy only to those with a POW fetish. I don't say this because I am spitting sour grapes or toeing a party line; I say this because guys say this. Guys say this to me all the time. When guys see these girls out here, in the real world (a world where most guys, by their own admission, are obsessed with the *round* parts of a woman—boobs and butts), they are repulsed by these girls, with the exception of a few very sick individuals whose sexual fantasies involve broken hip bones and crushed clavicles. The best compliment I ever heard a guy come up with for these girls (and I use the word *compliment* very loosely, as this is not something I'd like to have said about me, as it is both derogatory and uses the f-word, which by its nature can never be *that* complimentary) is "I would fuck her." He *would* fuck her, as in, "If I were starving within an inch of my mortal life, I *would* eat human flesh." "If I were trapped in solitary confinement for several weeks, I *would sleep* in my own waste." "If I had been lost in the wilderness for several years, I *would* watch *Trading Spaces*."

So how do we look at these images? Through what prism do we define what they mean and how they affect what we do, how we think about ourselves, how we live our lives? Because, really, we can't deny that they do affect us, every girl and woman on this continent, and anybody who says differently is clearly delusional, or a liar, or living off the grid on a communal habitation compound somewhere where they wear hemp clothing and sprout garbanzo beans in the little window greenhouse over the sink and sprinkle flax seed on things and make their own tofu. And it's okay if they affect us, they just can't be allowed to dominate how we think. The more time you spend obsessing about how you wish you were more like the girls in the magazines, the less time you're spending having a freaking life, for chrissake. And that's really what it's all about, no? You, having the best time you can, kicking ass and taking names, not hesitating to think about whether you'd be having more fun if your lip gloss color was from this season instead of last season? (Let me take the suspense out of it for you: you wouldn't. Lip gloss is most fun when it is being eaten, drunk, or kissed off. In all three of these scenarios, the nature and hue of the pigment suspended therein is, most decidedly, moot.)

Here's the prescription: first, we have to see this stuff as conceptual. It is not meant to be a recipe, a scheme for living, a set of instructions. My mom (like every other mom in the Western Hemisphere—what'd they have, a newsletter?) used to always trot out that old saw about "If you saw (insert name of influential person here, usually a very popular girl or that excellent boy in the tenth grade who had muscles and was pretty like a girl) jump off the Empire State Building, would you?" And I would sniff "No, of course not, and what does that have to do with getting my nose pierced or making out with a boy in the basement at Jenny Burns' house?" Well, that's what we're doing. We're jumping. We're watching others engaged in extreme physical behavior and we're running right up behind them, going "Me too! Me too! I want to starve myself into oblivion! I want to get my lips injected with creepy necrotized fat globules that have been extracted from my ass! I want to pay a thousand bucks to have my hair straightened in a chemically-driven heat process that is sure to make me look like a mange-ridden street urchin from nineteenth-century London."[43]

I think this is the perfect time in this one-sided conversation to mention Martha Stewart. She could not be more perfectly illustrative of the point I am trying (in a very verbose and slightly roundabout way) to make here. I don't say this because she had this seemingly perfect life that thousands of women tried, pathetically, desperately, frustratingly, to emulate, only to find that it was all a gingerbread façade, a *croquembouche* tower of sand, a thin veneer of caramelized sugar hiding the fetid, curdled crème of rage, deception, and stock-market manipulation below.

I say this because the rest of us, the sane ones anyway, never did try to emulate Martha. There was a period, a good long period a few years ago, when I read *Martha Stewart Living* quite regularly (it was a dark, difficult time for me; I was going through some personal changes). I suppose that *read* is really too strong for what I did with that magazine. *Scan,* was more like it, or *ogle* or even *ooooo.* I looked at the pictures. I looked at the pictures, and they

43. They used to dump their chamberpots out the window onto the heads of passersby. *Lots* of mange going around back then.

were pretty, and enticing, and a bit mysterious, since no matter how detailed the recipes and instructions and diagrams were, I still couldn't quite figure out how any of that shit got done. So I would look at the photos, and lick my lips, and rub my tummy, then go make myself a peanut butter and jelly sandwich and think how nice it would be to have a staff of browbeaten peons to dip almonds in liquid silver or pull the wings off hummingbirds or dismantle a thousand roses and reassemble it into one monstrous, unholy rose. Not once, *not once*, did I think, "Why don't I skip out and try to find a thousand heirloom English cottage roses and spend the next thirty-six hours pulling them apart and then gluing them back together?" The thought never crossed my mind. And you know why? Because it shouldn't have. That magazine is *just* to look at, to admire, to marvel at and shake one's head in bafflement, to fling across the room in disgust, then to pull out the photos and take them to someone else and have *those* suckers assemble the twelve-foot almond fluff cake tower with gold leaf and tiny operable marzipan violins. No one is trying to copy Martha's entire lifestyle as documented in that accursed rag. It's impossible, *even for her*.[44] At most, we might try to make that one, simple (Martha prefers the word *rustic*—she

44. Martha's life, as has been well-documented and thoroughly parodied, is propped up by a massive, writhing, human machine, churning out activities and projects and arts and crafts and concoctions and confections and distressed sidetables at an astounding rate. It is a pyramid of human flesh, with slaves upon peons upon lackeys upon whipping boys, and at the very bottom, the untouchable of the untouchables: production assistants.

AISHA TYLER

always has to make everything *so* fancy) fruit tartlet, the one you pick because it's *supposed* to look kind of lumpy and jagged, as if it might have fallen to the floor mid-construction, to make for our friend's birthday, or bridal shower, or breakup fête. We don't look at her (meaning-less) photo essay on heirloom eggs (which consists of, I kid you not, pages and pages of pictures of—you guessed it—*eggs*; it was like porn for farmers) and immediately run out and try to raise a flock of araucana chickens. Who the *hell* raises chickens?

And second (hah! I bet you thought I forgot), we have to see it as funny. Realize that it is entertainment, meant to be ironic, titillating, wry, provocative, and, finally, art. Art is to be contemplated, observed, interpreted, admired, burned during a country's cultural dark period, printed onto postcards, silkscreened onto T-shirts, auctioned off for pennies at estate fire sales, and copied and hung in midpriced hotel chains across the country. It is not meant to be taken literally, and it is definitely not meant to be turned into some kind of kooky life plan by the gullible and easily impressioned. If you can see the comedy, the hi-larity, the general lack of substance in this stuff, it will cease to affect you as gospel. It will just be another form of enjoyment, like Häagen-Dazs ice cream bars or bathtub masturbation.

I admit quite wholeheartedly that I read fashion maga-zines, and am, at times, quite seduced by them. But a good amount of the time, *most* of the time, I look at them for what they are: not the Bible, not an instruction booklet, just a big book full of pictures of people who in person look like influenza survivors, wearing a lot of stuff I wish I owned but would probably spill a plate of spaghetti[45] or a Blue Hawaiian on within minutes of getting dressed and ruin it forever, thus forcing myself to go back to wearing sweatpants, flip-flops, and men's white undershirts from Target. Which, in case you didn't know, is the newest in slob chic.

45. A word I wish would come back into the lexicon. If your noodles are covered in red sauce of any kind, weren't made by hand, and don't have anything unholy mixed in, like squid ink or flower petals, it's spaghetti. Simple as that. It was good enough when you were a kid, and it's damn good enough now.

It's Your Turn to Clean the Pole

or

Why Everyone Should Learn a Vocation

I am done with strip clubs. For real. No more.

Not that I was ever some kind of massive patron of the gentleman's club. I am straight, and a girl, and, as such, not a prime target for the exotic dancing industry. But strangely enough I have found myself, on more than one occasion, sitting in a dark and faintly damp pleather banquette in the corner of a joint called Crazy Girls or Crazy Horse or Crazy Butterfly.[46] Which I don't quite understand,

---

46. It seems that, for some reason, lapsed mental capacity figures greatly into men's perceptions of the kind of girl who would take her clothes off in front of a roomful of strangers. Why that is I don't know, because guys' most common dismissal of a girl who is behaving in a way that is no longer convenient to them (i.e., she wants a commitment; is tired of having furtive, split-second sex with him at three in the morning after a drunk booty call; is pissed that she found him in bed with her seventeen-year-old cousin) is to call them a *psycho*. The fact that this is an insult is a mystery, as guys seem to think of crazy girls as hot. Hence the ever-popular strip club name, Crazy Girls. Why would you want to spend a night stuffing dollar bills into the underpants of

because a much better descriptor would be Never-Finished-High-School Girls, or Short-on-Cash-but-Long-on-Boobs Ladies, or Trying-to-Feed-a-Killer-Pot-Habit Foxes, or Supporting-Three-Illegitimate-Kids-and-a-Freeloading-Slob-of-a-Boyfriend—Live and Nude Onstage!

Every time I find myself in one of these places, I usually spend the first few minutes frantically trying to retrace my steps, to deduce just how it is I came to find myself in a room where black lights and neon accents aren't intended ironically, where guys are squawking "Hell, yeah" as if they were at a rock concert while trying to avoid eye contact with each other, and two girls are bobbing up and down on the neck of some hapless rube in a folding chair as if they are trying to choke him to death, to end his life in a grand theatrical death-by-angry-crotch.

Eventually I give up, order a drink (usually some type of malt liquor beverage, which seems most appropriate), and try to enjoy myself as best I can, which usually means trying to learn something, glean *some* meaning from the experience on behalf of all my gender. It's my responsibility, I tell myself, as I drink my third Zima. I am a reporter, a sociologist, a spy. I will figure all this out and report back to my fellow girls at the next meeting. I will expose this, debunk it, crack all this open. I will blow the roof off of this whole strip-club phenomenon once and for all. I am not

_____

girls who are in the same mental state as your enraged ex-girlfriend? What kind of fucked-up shit is that?

seduced by this. I don't find it funny. The human seesaw double-frontal crotchal attack does not dazzle me. I am a sober, analytical eye. *I am going to figure this whole thing out.*

But whenever I am in a strip club, I find myself reacting in all kinds of peculiar and inappropriate ways. Ways I would not expect. First let me say that as a rule, I have always felt quite sorry for strippers. I feel sad that they have to take off their clothes for a living, and in a place that smells like hotdog water and Coors Light, and I feel sad that they have to wear those shoes with the platform soles and the see-through Lucite heels.[47] I feel sad that they have to get surgery to make their boobs so big even Pamela Anderson would wince and exhale "Wow, that's a bit much." I feel sad that they have to grind all around in front of a room full of knuckleheads and itinerant truckers. And worst of all, I feel sad that none of them stayed in school and learned a skill. I have always felt, very deeply, that if they could only type seventy words per minute, they wouldn't have had to resort to such a humiliating, soul-rending profession.

As a result, the first time I went to a strip club, I felt *very* sad, a little angry and indignant, and wanted to gather them all up at once, all of these bruised fruit and wilted

47. In what other industry are those shoes useful? None. If you are making or buying shoes with a Lucite heel, you are a denizen of the stripping underworld. Either that or you're a porn star. Or a pimp with questions of gender identity.

flowers, stuff them in a van, Lucite shoes and pneumatic boobs and all, and take them down to the local community college for some remedial classes. I imagined some of them wouldn't want to go, and would complain, or try to scratch me, or hiss like a kitty when you try to give it a bath, even though you coo at it and pet it to let it know you mean it no harm. But I would remain resolute, because I would know I was doing the right thing. I would take them all down to the city college, and pay for all of their courses. I would offer to tutor them, and spend time on the phone giving pep talks and encouragement, and come back months later and stand proudly by when they get their G.E.D. certificates, maybe handing out paper cups of punch or juice boxes to commemorate their big day, their transition into a mainstream, respectable life, their "going legit."

But when I got inside, my feelings changed. Because here's the thing: *I'm not sure all of these women realize that this is a bad job to have.* I'm sure many of them do, and smoke and drink a lot to cover up the fact that their job sucks, and that they are being exploited, and that there are predators who will try to take advantage of them, and that strip clubs don't have 401(k) plans. But a lot of them seemed just fine, all bubbly and cheery and perfectly normal, and not at all hangdog or teary or sullen like I expected. I go in every time thinking that the club will be like some kind of human veal pen, the girls looking up with giant, dewy eyes like some awful pop art painting, and dancing around like marionettes, or like one of those toys made out of wood and elastic, where you push the bottom of the base and they fall to one side and then stand back up again, suddenly at attention, all painted-on smile and rigid little arms.

Except instead of a factory-farm chicken coop, I find an aviary. The women are flitting about, having conversations about hair color and gym memberships and what happened that week on *ER*. They sit down and talk with me (*only* talk, because clearly I am not there for a lap dance. I am not in a strip club to see naked ladies. I could do that at home) and tell me that they're paying their way through college, or trying to save enough money to open a bar, or move to New York, or buy a house. And they have all their teeth and don't seem to have been kicked in the head, and aren't lisping or looking around nervously for Tiny the four-hundred-pound Enforcer to come around and twist their arms and make them say, in a tiny, quavering voice, that "this club is a very nice place to work."

I once had a girl who was dressed adorably, in a tropical bathing suit and matching miniskirt, with a little lunchbox as a purse (which went out around the time it became funny rather than cool to listen to bands like Siouxsie and the Banshees but nevertheless worked for her) sit down and ask me if I wanted to buy her a drink. Once I established that "buying her a drink" wasn't secret code for some kind of high-priced service like a double-team lap dance or the aforementioned crotchal attack, I agreed. I had never "bought a drink" for a girl before, and it made me feel instantly mack-like. Sipping her drink, she pulled out a pack of American Spirit cigarettes and told me she wasn't going to dance anymore that night. She was going to sit and drink with me until it was time to go home. I asked her if some bald guy with a stack of fleshy rolls at the back of his neck and an eye tic wouldn't come over and rough her up. She said no, she came and went as she pleased, danced only as much as she wanted to, could say no to anyone at any time, and that the only thing the security was there for was to throw out guys who refused to pay or tried to grab ... *things*. I don't know if it was the Long Island Iced Tea (never, never again, I swear) but I couldn't quite grasp it. I asked her if she just showed up whenever, and left whenever, and did whatever she wanted, how did she make any money? She told me that the girls kept everything they made, and the club made money on the door and drinks. I imagined her counting her twenty-seven dollars in sweaty ones, maybe ironing them until they were shiny and crisp and putting them in a shoebox under her bed at night, dreaming of the day she'd have enough to move into an apartment with hot running water. She then proceeded to open that silly little lunchbox of a purse. Enough money spilled out of it to make Daffy Duck scream "Mine! Mine! Mine! Down! Down! Down! It's all mine!" She puffed on her natural tobacco cigarette, took a sip of her drink (that I instantly regretted buying her, considering she was clearly much, much richer than me), and purred, "I made three thousand dollars tonight."

I fainted.

How unnerving. How infuriating. I go in expecting suffering, misery, a human veal pen, and what I get is butterfly wings and bags of money. It throws me all off, kicks sand in the face of all my ideas about the exploitation of women and psychosexual politics and the unknowing female complicity in our own subjugation and how everyone thinks just like me and, if they don't, well then, goddammit, they should.

Of course, there are many, *many* women who have been victimized in one way or another (some of whom are so messed up in the head they don't even realize it), and are in the sex industry because they know nothing else, or have been forced in, who feel as if they have no other options. There are women who were abused as children, or as adults, who have a wholly unnatural relationship to their sexuality, and to men's perception of their sexuality, or who only feel valuable when they are being degraded or objectified by other people. There are plenty of these women in strip clubs all over the country, and there are plenty of strip clubs that are awful, filthy, degrading, depressing, even dangerous places to work.[48] But, I'm sad-slash-sorry to say,

> SWERVE

48. Which is why we girls should pay more, not less, attention to these places, to make them safer for the girls that work there.

a bunch of these women seem perfectly, totally, frustratingly . . . *normal.*

Which is why I think every woman should try to understand the world of exotic dancing a little better. Because it's less skeevy than you expect. And because these are *real* women, women who deserve the compassion of other women rather than their derision. And most important, because guys are fascinated by it. Riveted, obsessed, stopped short in their tracks, eyes glazed over, mouths agape, at the vision, glimpse, or even suggestion of naked ladies dancing around on a narrow dais with dollar bills hanging out of their underwear.[49] And it can be icky, and creepy, and depressing and disgusting to us, or we can try to get comfortable with it, get some grasp of it, figure what it is that makes it so unbelievably fascinating to guys. Because, the truth is, it's fascinating to quite a few women as well. Five minutes in a male strip show in full gyratory swing will make you think that girls are by far the more doglike of the genders. *Woof.*

49. I was having drinks with a friend a while back and asked him why it is that guys love booby bars so much. For some reason, he couldn't answer me just then. He admitted that it can be very uncomfortable, and more than a little depressing, to watch girls dance around naked in front of a room of clammy-palmed knuckleheads drinking watered-down Jack and Cokes. But he still maintained that there was something enjoyable about it, something that overwhelmed all of the creepy elements. He just couldn't articulate exactly what it was. As fate would have it, he was planning on going to a booby bar later, so he promised me he'd think on it and get back to me. That night at about eleven I got a drunken cell-phone call during which he gave me a surprisingly intellectual analysis of why men love to go to topless joints. It had

Naked = Dancing?

What is it about the human psyche that makes us enjoy watching people dance around naked? Why do we enjoy seeing members of the opposite sex rip off poorly constructed, ill-fitting dirty schoolgirl and naughty construction worker outfits and toss them into the air with abandon while simultaneously doing a godawful version of the cabbage patch? Why do we risk public embarrassment and possible intestinal distress by watching these "dancers" while wolfing down lukewarm chicken wings in a room that hasn't been redecorated or disinfected since the Nixon presidency? *What is that about?*

We know that most of us are interested in sex. With other people. Which most of us, most of the time, can't get in any satisfactory amount. So it stands to follow that we'd be interested in naked other people. Yes. Fine. So why aren't we content to watch a naked person just stand there, like a model for a painting class? Why doesn't da Vinci's famous anatomical illustration make our mouths water? The guy's got four arms, for chrissake. Think of all the happy spots he could find. *At once.*

If the standing thing doesn't do it for us, why don't they just lie there? If the whole point is to look at something that approximates sex when we can't have it, why

something to do with the reptile brain, the vestigial core of our animal id, the impetus for human survival, and our psychic relationship to the primeval jungle. I was quite impressed, until he ended his diatribe by stating that he planned to punch out the guy he was with in order to "grab this girl with an ass like a peach." I thought that was taking the scenario a bit too far.

not just look at a naked person lying there on the ground, perhaps wiggling and grunting a little bit like a slutty overturned turtle, and leave it at that? Oh no, we want our strangely naked people bobbing around uncomfortably, whipping off boas and ripping off Spandex while we whoop and holler in concert with other intoxicated strangers, our eyes forward to avoid catching the eye of another and suddenly realizing, in that moment, how truly mortifying and ridiculous this whole ritual is.

Now you're thinking smugly, "Well, that's just guys. Guys are the sicko horndogs who go and watch these freakshows. Us ladies, we knit and have tea and discuss mutual funds delicately over crustless sandwiches." Au contraire, *ma soeur*. I have had the strange pleasure of viewing a male strip show in a room full of women, and let me tell you, there is no more sexually objectifying, ass-smacking, high-pitched, eardrum shattering, twenty-dollar-bill-stuffing group than a room full of our genteel sex. We are animals. We grab, we throw drinks, we slap and pull and lick, we are monstrous. I have seen women grab male strippers around the neck in a sweaty death grip and drag them off stage. I have seen women stick their tongues down the throats of men who clearly had not been asked first, who seemed to be gasping for air, struggling for one last gulp of that sweet life's breath. This kind of behavior in a female strip club would get a man beaten within an inch of his life and tossed into a Dumpster. It happens so regularly with male strippers that after shows the guys compare injuries and strip shows have strict no-touching rules.

"Us? The fairer sex? Surely, you jest!" Surely, I do not. Leave your nose wrinkling and mockingly distasteful faces on the side table. We are as much culprits as men, if in smaller numbers. But why? What is it about the stripping experience that is so compelling? And what about the experience might be personally liberating?

I have been to several strip shows, and watched members of both genders *take it off, take it all off!* And I can say pretty confidently that guys and girls react to strip shows very differently. I'm no scientist—it's not statistically significant or anything. It's just what I think.

Guys usually act two ways when they are watching a strip show. If they are the kind of guys for whom a trip to a strip club is a once-in-a-blue-moon occasion, a real treat, like birthday cake or oral sex without reciprocation, they are elated. They yell, and clap their friends on the back, and laugh, and whoop *whoo!* and *yeah!* and *she's hot!* and the event is a group bonding activity, with all of the guys feeling as if they have had a liberating, exciting, transcendent experience, one that brought them together, much like a long ski weekend or nearly drowning on an ill-fated whitewater rafting trip.

If, on the other hand, this is something they do often, perhaps alone, in a place where the bartenders and bouncers know them by name, or they have a special table, or a favorite dancer, they are decidedly less animated. They stare forward, eyes on the girls at all times. Their mouths may fall open, and drool or spittle of some kind may escape. They keep their hands where people can see them, so as not to give the impression that they are touching themselves, although their facial expression indicates they are engaged in some kind of furious mental masturbation, trying to use brainwaves to get their business done without actually having to reach down. They don't laugh, or clap anyone on the back. Their look is serious, scowling, business-like. If they do look you in the eye, it seems as if they might be trying to hypnotize you. It's best to look away, lest you be drawn into the deathray of their mental self-pleasuring. These are the people who give strip clubs their unique creepiness.

A guy friend of mine told me about his bachelor party, for which several of his friends hired a stripper. They weren't in a strip club, they were in someone's house, which should have made it more comfortable, more *homey*, I suppose. But whenever you see someone take off their clothes and gyrate herkily to a ZZ Top song from a portable beat box in the middle of someone's starkly lit, futon furnished, shag carpeted living room, it illustrates perfectly why strip clubs are dark and lit only by neon and the gleam of the brass pole, and maybe a few flashing colored

AISHA TYLER

strobes right when someone rips off their tearaway pants. It's weird, uncomfortable, even a little comical. All the guys sat there, in The Position: stiffly rigid, faces forward, mouths open, saliva collecting at the corners, hands placed, palms sweatily down on kneecaps, glassy eyes blinking sporadically, as if any movement at all would indicate emotion, create some *moment* that would then have to be laughed away later when the drinking began in earnest to fill up the gaping hole left by the departure of Dancing Naked Girl. My friend actually gave the Position some sound effects: a kind of cartoonish *"floink! floink!"* for the blinks, and a faint trickling sound—*"blobble, blobble"*—for the drooling. He said that was all you could hear in that room for the entire time she was dancing around the man of the hour, seated regally on the futon couch. That, and ZZ Top. And apparently, for that group of men, the uncomfortable silence was completely comfortable. It is better not to speak or make any kind of ocular or physical contact, than to have the accidental glance or brush of a hand proclaim to the entire room that you are aroused, and despite the presence of a perfectly good half-naked pirouetting female, you would rather focus your sexual energies on your male neighbor. It is this paralyzing fear of being branded gay when you aren't, or more to the point, when you are and haven't yet admitted it to others, or yourself, that keeps men at silent, slackjawed, zombielike attention when boobs are ranging freely about the room. This is not behavior that seems natural for this type of situation, but for guys, it seems to work just fine.

Women, on the other hand, have no such fears. We don't care if people call us gay. In fact, quite the opposite—we regularly engage in behavior that would reinforce precisely such an opinion. Who cares? Lesbians aren't threatening, they're sexy. They're modern. They're a primary component of most pornographic motion pictures. Lesbians are the new black.

So we hug repeatedly, hold hands, sit with our arms around each other, kiss each other on the cheeks, and sometimes on the lips. We compliment each other's stomachs, and butts, and boobs, and lips, and have no reservation about staring into another woman's eyes and telling her how incredibly sexy she is, and how anyone would be lucky to have her. This kind of behavior, if directed toward a guy, would have him dusting off the circa 1989 condoms in his wallet. Essentially, normal, platonic, friendly behavior between female friends is just a constant series of passes. This social freedom, this lack of inhibition, makes us a fearsome strip club audience.

Grokdar the Horse-Hung, or size does matter, but not in the way you think

HBO has a long-running documentary series called *Real Sex*, the main purpose of which, as far as I can tell, is to embarrass people. It's ostensibly a show documenting the sexual behaviors of normal people—"normal" meaning people who like to spank each other while wearing latex pantsuits and squatting on top of some kind of water-wheel/penis machine invented by two creepy, grinning, preternaturally skinny Germans. Under the guise of being a documentary show, which most people mistakenly interpret as a "news" show (which of course, implies objectivity and thus *commands* divulgence),[50] the producers are able to get normal, everyday couples on the street to freely admit to having engaged in all kinds of kinky and deeply embarrassing sexual activities (threesomes; orgies; fingers in bad places; screaming; biting; spanking; weeping; Sleepy, Grumpy and Doc; and poo sports). That is the first element of "real sex." The second is longform stories about people who have turned these activities into a hobby, or an avocation, or a multimillion-dollar sex empire, or at least into a semiannual poo festival at the neighborhood vegan coffee shop. Apparently one of the requirements for turning your lifelong obsession with poo into a lucrative franchise is being gruesomely comfortable with being naked in front of strangers (although I guess if you love poo, you are probably not inhibited about much else), and so we get plenty of eyefuls of fifty-seven-year-old nude performance artists reciting love poetry while lighting their farts. That sup-

50. And of course, the two couldn't be more different: just ask Charlton Heston about *Bowling for Columbine*. From what I could tell, he thought he would be talking to an objective reporter, to whom he could rationally make the NRA's case, when he agreed to be interviewed by Michael Moore. Of course, he also thought it was 1967 and he was the Queen of England.

posedly, is the other element of "real sex." I suppose there is nothing more real than lighting your own gaseous emissions. I mean, you could die. Or at least burn your bottom really badly.

Anyway, one particularly absorbing episode of *Real Sex*[51] had an illuminating segment on an all-male strip team from Philadelphia. They were a very special team, a *troupe*, if you will, in that they always stripped down to nothing (unlike those pussies at Chippendales, who go prancing around the stage in G-strings made up like tiny tuxedos, which is neither ironic nor really that sexy, just frustrating and mildly effete). They stripped down to nothing, and their nothing was so . . . *a whole lot of something*, that they were the single most popular all-male strip troupe on all of the eastern seaboard. These guys were well-endowed in the same way that the Hummer gets low gas mileage: to state that fact is to miss the point entirely. They are medical miracles, walking cartoons, porn stars on hiatus, sideshow performers. If, like the X-Men, you consider a genetic misfire a gift, these men would all be superheroes. When you are operating at their level, it ceases being about sex, and starts to be about spectacle.

The women who attend these shows know this, and behave accordingly. They know they are there to see something unusual, something special, something eyepoppingly

---

51. *Real Sex 20*, I believe, for those of you who will rush out immediately after reading the next paragraph to do some investigative research of your own.

absurd, and they are ready. They are a bloodthirsty herd, a passel of raving lunatics. They scream, they cry, emit guttural noises, wave money like angry pimps, demanding that the guys come grind on them *right now, get over here, you, big poppa, I'm talking to you!* These men are pawed to within an inch of their lives, squeezed, grabbed, pulled, slapped, grabbed, rubbed as if a stripper's ass meant good luck, as if a genie might pop out and make them nineteen-year-old millionaires. There is no uncomfortable silence, no stock-still eyes-forward stares, no *floink! floink!* no *blobble! blobble!* There is nothing but screaming and shoving and high-pitched squeals of glee, of release, of women finally doing what they have wanted to do for so very long—to objectify men, to put them on the spot, completely unadorned, and *smack that ass.*

Here's the thing I found most poignant about this whole story. These guys cannot find underwear capacious enough to shroud their uniquely voluminous groins. They have taken, as a group, most of whom are straight, to making their own G-strings, on a sewing machine that they take with them on tour. Some of them were quite handy with a needle and thread, and had an array of flashy underthings in a variety of fabrics—sequins, silk, lamé—all the strip-friendly textiles. To the women, these guys are horse-hung sexoholics. But in their quiet moments, these men are just normal guys, trying to find a nice pair of well-fitting underwear.

* * *

I want to say that if there are any guys reading this, whether gay, straight, or bicurious, that you should not, for a second, feel intimidated. No woman (or man) actually wants a guy with these kinds of endowments. We are not laying awake at night dreaming of Grokdar the Horse-Hung. There is a point at which you pass from indulgence into pure gluttony. When Dagwood Bumstead would make those seventeen-decker sandwiches, did you think he was actually going to be able to eat them? Did anyone believe (Dagwood included) that he could fit his lips around a sandwich roughly the height of his entire torso? No. He would take that monstrosity into the living room, and when we were distracted by a panel of Blondie hanging out the wash or baking a batch of mini-quiches for her joint catering venture with Tootsie Woodley, he would dismantle the sandwich and eat it in more sensible, manageable portions. While it may be quite titillating to *look* at a four-foot-tall sandwich, no one wants to put one in their mouth. Or anywhere else, for that matter.

If you pay attention to most women's sandwich-eating habits, we tend to be seduced by delicious but relatively diminutive concoctions. Baguettes with brie. Focaccia panini. Tea sandwiches. We like a nice open-faced cucumber tower or a salmon rectangle, maybe egg salad with some parsley. We are not running around town with four-foot meatball subs or Cotto salami hoagies. We like a nice, tasty, *manageable* sandwich. Sometimes with the crusts cut off. It is much more important to us how the sandwich is presented, and what it's filled with, and how long it takes us to eat it, and whether it comes with dessert, than how big the sandwich is itself. If we have to choose, we'd rather have the entire tea service than just one big meat-and-cheese-filled brute of a grinder.

You getting me? Really, this sandwich metaphor can only go so far.

Having had the dubious pleasure of attending both male and female strip shows, I am convinced that girls, on the whole, are the more offensive and outrageous of the two sexes when it comes to group behavior. Unlike heterosexual girls, though, you will never find a straight guy in a male strip venue. I suspect this is because a large part of the adult hetero male's energy is spent trying to avoid proximity with the reproductive organs of other adult males. Which is too bad, because I think guys could learn a lot about women, and about themselves, by attending a male strip show. But that will never happen, so I won't even begin holding my breath. The penis is like an evil talisman, human garlic, warding off all heterosexual males who might hope to enter. If you were ever trying to keep a creepy guy away from you, and you could engineer some kind of situation in which he'd have no choice but to pass by another male penis to get to you, you could be reasonably confident that you wouldn't have to worry about him turning up ever again.

Of course, this has been done successfully many times. It's called the rebound boyfriend.

Way to Be Inappropriate

Sometimes, at parties, people like to play this game, where they ask everyone to sit in a circle. If you are ever at a party, and people ask you to sit in a circle, get out right away, because either they're going to play a stupid game, or they're going to try to brainwash you into joining their cult. Either way, you're in for a really boring time, so hightail it out of there pronto.

Any game in which you sit in a circle is lame, but one of the lamest is the one where everyone has to tell an embarrassing story about themselves. First of all, it's not really a game, because you can't win anything, unless you count grand humiliation in front of a group of your peers a prize. It's more like a contest to see who is the biggest numbskull, and I figure you could deduce that yourself if you waited until everyone was good and drunk to see who fell down, threw up, or started a fistfight.

I actually have a friend who won this game quite hand- ily, by recounting how she drank too much and passed out in the bedroom at someone's house during a party. This, in and of itself, is not particularly spectacular. What put it over the top was that it was a party filled with people she worked with. And she fell asleep on top of everyone's coats. When she woke up, they were all gone, which meant that one by one, each and every colleague of hers came, lifted some part of her body, limbs or torso, head or bottom, and gingerly removed their coat, getting a nice snorey whiff of whatever combination of alcoholic beverages she was mix- ing that night. As far as I'm concerned, *that* is a cool story. She's the queen of the party foul in my book. Which isn't such a bad thing, because you get to wear a crown and scepter and order people to go get you beers and stuff.

Anyhoo, I have "won" this game exactly one time, if again, *winning* means splaying out the darkest, most acrid parts of my past for others to inspect and mock. Before I tell you how I won, I will say that I could win this game all the time, if I so chose, because as poised and sophisticated as I aspire to be, I am now, and have been for many years, a six-foot-tall girl. While this may seem like an asset, what with the comparisons to a model and the ability to get cookies down off the topmost shelves and all, when I was a kid of say, fourteen, and all the boys were like tiny elves, scurrying about and making fun of me from somewhere around my ankles, it was not so much. You may also think of tall women as naturally graceful, like gazelles stooping to delicately sip from the waters of the Serengeti. Nothing could be further from the truth. We are like newborn fawns, Bambis on ice, skittering about, bumping into everything and everyone within range, toppling bookshelves and crushing tiny Smurftowns in our wake. I have ceased to be surprised or even upset when I burn myself on the oven, or tumble down the stairs, or cut myself with a knife, or a scissors, or a scrap of paper, or a spear of asparagus. I have put my finger into my own eye several times, without any apparent external influences, such as someone pushing me, or a poltergeist. While this might confuse or enrage some, I have made my peace with it. I have resigned myself to a life of creative injury.

So when I say I could win this game all the time, it is not an idle threat. It is a promise.

For the sake of my own dignity and the esteem of others, I keep most of these awful episodes to myself (better to share them only with the few eyewitnesses and the tiny, mortified Aisha inside my head). Which is why I have "won" the "game" only once. It wasn't even the worst thing that's ever happened to me. But it was a doozy.

I was out with a group of friends in high school, one of which was the grand love of my life at that time. Huge crush. He knew it too, and kept infuriatingly cool, which only made me pine for him more. Upon reflection, I realize that he was kind of a dick for not either making a move or telling me I never had a chance but, back then, all I could see was his great smile and his parachute pants. (Back then, they were cool. Judge not, lest ye Members Only jacket be judged.) I was smitten. Being smitten, if you're not quite sure, entails mooning over said Crush instead of paying attention in class, spending way too much time over at friends' houses who live in Crush's neighborhood in order to possibly catch a glimpse of Crush, and indiscriminately telling all of Crush's friends that one likes Crush, so that Crush feels self-conscious and hunted every time you are in the same room with Crush and anyone else who knows about how you feel, which in my case, was all of my high school and most of the three surrounding ones.

Yet and still, Crush seemed to like me enough, and we shared the same circle of friends, so we were all out on this particular evening, in someone's crappy car. In high school, *all* cars were crappy—*hooptie* was the vernacular for junkbox ride at the time—but because they were all equally crappy, you would judge someone on how much less crappy their car was than someone else's. This was how the coolness food chain was constructed. If you were cool enough to get a crappy old European car, like a jillion-year-old BMW 2000 series, or (god forbid—this was mine) an Opel, you leapt up like four levels on the food chain, simply because you were ballsy enough to spend your entire summer job savings on a car that you would never be able to find any parts for. As a result, you did a lot of partying in your car, because you never knew when you would have to abandon it by the side of the road for the city to deal with.

So we were in some junkbox hooptie, doing what high school kids do in the park in someone's car, which is a) make fun of each other, or b) drink. I would love to say that I never had a beer in high school, but hey, this isn't a Scholastic book, so why don't I just drop the act, hm? I was the wine-cooler queen.

On this particular night, in this particular car, I had had a beer or two, and was trying to be as scintillating as possible toward Crush, while simultaneously ridiculing another friend mercilessly for his poor taste in music (Ready for the World) and his poor taste in clothing (acid wash). He may have also had a Jheri Curl, but let's not malign the poor man's character too much when he's not here to defend himself, okay?

I was starting to really have to pee, which was keeping me from being either as scintillating or as insulting as I would have liked to have been, and I felt my game was coming off. So I got out of the car and hiked down the trail we were parked on, planning to have a little secret rendezvous with nature,[52] then return triumphant to the hooptie,

52. Do not wrinkle your nose at me, little lady. If you have not peed outside, then you are either an English royal or a bedridden invalid. Everyone in the world has done this. Some people in the world have *no choice* but to do this. What kind of First World toilet snob *are* you?

replete with new insults for Mr. Ready for the World and charming new tidbits for Crush.

I hiked down the trail a long way. Really. At least, I thought I did. It felt like I did, but my mind was addled with visions of kissing Crush and a bit of the Mickey's Big Mouth, and maybe my sense of distance was all off. I got to what I thought was a good place, daintily assumed the position, and got down to business.

There is a time, during "business," where there is no turning back. Catch it early, or catch it late, and you can abort the mission for a better time. Catch it in the middle, and you have no choice but to deliver your payload. It was at this precise time in my military operation that the brain surgeon in the hooptie chose to turn on his headlights.

Shit, I thought, *I shouldn't have said that last thing about the acid-wash jacket making him look like a male hooker from Scranton,* as the headlights fully illuminated the choicest parts of my anatomy, rendered especially visible by the yogalike crouch I had chosen.

When I got back to the car, having first crab-walked out of the klieg lights, jeans around my calves, finished the job, and composed myself, everyone insisted they couldn't see anything. *You were too far away, the lights were too bright, it might have seemed as if we were lighting up your bum like a shiny Christmas turkey, but that was just an optical illusion* . . . In my overwhelming desire to maintain the delicate (im)balance of power between myself and Crush, I chose to believe them. Even though I knew they were lying, those Jordache wearing, faux Prince-pop liking, malt-liquor-breath-having turncoats. I knew they were lying. And they proved it to me years later by describing in excruciating detail the hills and valleys of my caramel posterior, down to the birthmark. By that time, I had come into my own, fully resigned to bear the burden of my inelegant misfortune, so it didn't come as much of a blow.[53]

And Crush? Ah, the Crush. After that it was never quite the same. The luster came off Crush, and his shiny parachute pants, and I ended up falling in love with a potter/graffiti artist who dedicated his murals to me. No better way to make a girl love you than to break the law in her honor.

I think we humans are drawn to self-immolation. We crave embarrassment, savor humiliation, subconsciously pursue ridicule. We are like extreme athletes of ignominy, teetering precipitously on the razor's edge of propriety. We look danger in the face, its eyes flaming, fangs bared, breath fetid, reeking of brimstone and the stink of public shame, and we shrug our shoulders, titter and bleat, "I think it's *entirely* appropriate for me to have sex with my boss on his desk during an all-office staff meeting. Don't look at me with those flaming eyes!" Maybe it makes us feel more authentic somehow, more alive, to bleed from self-inflicted wounds to the psyche. How else to explain the constant and unwavering effort by people to screw shit up?

53. . . . . I like to tell myself.

Hot sex on a blotter

I can sum up my philosophy on workplace sex thusly: don't shit where you sleep.[54] Unless you are planning on quitting, and so think nothing of being caught *in flagrante delicto*, ass upwards on tomorrow's sales report, being taught the do's and don'ts (a lesser person would have used the phrase "ins and outs" but I am a better girl than that) of a PowerPoint presentation by the unit manager, it's not the career move. Sleeping with a coworker inevitably ends badly. People question your integrity, your ability, your judgment, or worse, they start hitting on you because they figure you're the kind of girl who likes to spread it around the cube space. Your authority will forever come into question: people will assume you slept your way into that midlevel executive job with the long hours and nominal medical coverage, no matter how many times you send out e-mails from your workstation on Saturdays to prove you actually *do* work. The main problem is that people are awful. Awful, people. They talk, they whisper, they point and gawk, they tell stories and if those aren't exciting enough, they make stories up and tell those. Mind you, these people are probably not actively out to ruin your life. Think of them more like hyenas. If you never left a piece of rotting carrion by the side of the road, they wouldn't surround your house, nip at your hindquarters, and carry away all your goats. So keep it in your pants.

54. This strikes me as an axiom that can be applied to every aspect of one's life.

If you simply *must* have at that junior ad exec with the sweet ass, then you must find out first whether he can be discreet. Even nice boys sometimes lose verbal control when they are under the influence of alcohol and a long streak of regular sex. This is why one-night stands after office parties should be renamed "opportunities for me to rethink my career priorities and revise my resumé," because that is surely what you will be doing after ol' Blabbermouth Iwassodrunk from the second floor hits the pub after work with his cronies. Remember, all it takes is one e-mail, my friend. *One* e-mail.

Boom Chicka Pow Pow

We as women have to find a way to embrace, or at least understand, some aspect of the porn industry. It is very true that it is exploitive and demeaning, and many or even most of the women working in it are undereducated, self-hating and probably self-medicating. But it isn't going anywhere, and there is a whole area of the adult film industry that is entirely run by, and geared toward, women. If you're into it, it can be interesting. At the very least, it'll give you some great stories to tell at your next bridge game.

I think after the suffrage movement, the feminist movement, the sexual revolution, and the spectacular fall of Reverend Bakker, we must finally accept the truth: porn is here to stay. Despite all your hard stares and vigorous admonishments, regardless of the fact that the *minute* you were actually (finally!) broken up with your boyfriend you gleefully tossed his entire collection of vintage seventies porn on Beta, even though you close your eyes and hold your breath and wish and wish and wish . . . it ain't going anywhere. The best women can do is get to know it, understand it, and maybe make it a more illuminated world, so that women in it can be protected rather than exploited, that they can be treated fairly, and that the really horrible, exploitive stuff can be brought to light so we can stamp it out. Face it—*Maxim* is not the same as triple X snuff films. You can't lump it all together as "ick." If we understand it, if we own it even, we can change it. And have a pretty good time on a Saturday night too.

There are some companies run entirely by women that produce erotic films for women. I wouldn't know anything about them, because I've never come into contact with that stuff. I just heard about it from some guy in a Jamba Juice. Apparently it exists. You should check it out.

Starf**king

You know how they say that it's hard to find a San Francisco native actually still living in San Francisco? Well, it's hard to find a woman in Los Angeles who isn't trying her desperate, creaky best to sleep with a famous guy. If you aren't careful, you could suffocate in a sea of cleavage. It can be a bit annoying when you're at a bar trying to get a drink and some chick is grinding your backside because your hair looks just like Hugh Jackman's. This is why I always carry mace.

Women are of differing opinions on the subject of star sex. Some say that sleeping with someone just because they're famous is shallow and callous, and if you do it you'll get exactly what you deserve, namely a ruined dress and a few fun weeks in front of a congressional committee. I agree that starfucking is an empty and completely unfulfilling endeavor, but for different reasons. On the one hand, I do believe there is value in the beauty of the story; namely, if you can envision yourself out next Saturday night recounting your encounter in damp and minute detail, if you see yourself relishing the entire kiss-and-tell experience, and if you can divorce yourself completely from the idea that once you've slept with aforementioned famous guy he'll fall in love with you at once, dump ol' *Vanity Fair* cover whatshername and whisk you away to his summer mansion on Crete, well then by all means creep up to that suite at the Chateau Marmont and bang away. More power to you. Nothing better than acquisition sex, because the story's the thing.

And it had better be the thing, too, because I guarantee you, the sex will be *horrible*. Famous guys get sex thrown at them like fastballs in the major leagues. They have no reason to impress you—there's a line of willing nubiles fresh off the Greyhound forming a line in the hallway as soon as you close the door. Nonetheless, if that young, multimillion-dollar action star has made it clear that he holds a very special place for you in his pants, and you can't resist, go for it. I don't recommend it, but I won't judge. I'm not a judger.

Get in, get on, get down, get off, get up, get dressed, get out

It may surprise you to hear that I don't advocate one-night stands, as I seem to have dedicated at least a chapter to getting you hooked up. I don't. There's a whole rafter of reasons why; here are a few of the most persuasive (at least to me, at three in the morning on my fourth Red Bull).

- It is rare that a one-night stand is ever good. This is just a fact of nature, despite what your boozy girl-friends may wheeze at you late at night over one too many plum wines. On a one-night stand, one or both of you will probably be very drunk, which makes for teeth-grinding frustration for you, as you wait for the booze-delayed denouement that will never come, and butt-clenching frustration for him, as he waits for the jib to make it past three-quarter mast. Even a Jedi knight can't focus on the job at hand when he's got the added performance anxiety of trying to impress you while not embarrassing himself in the process. If by some holy intervention you enjoy yourself, you will unerringly find that when you wake, sober and chastened in the morning, it wasn't as good as you remember it, and you've got some lumpy friar of a guy in bed with you who couldn't possibly have been the hard body you brought home the night before.

- Just for kicks, let's say the sex was good. It is almost a certainty that you will not get to enjoy it again. Guys are notoriously fickle, and only want what they cannot have, or better yet, what they have to work bonebreakingly hard to get. Regardless of how ravishing you are when you wake up in the morning, or how lusciously seductive you were the night before, he will think to himself, "That was too easy. What's wrong with this broad?" He will then go ask his friends this same question, and they will roll through their shortlist of female maladies, finally settling on the catchall *psycho*, the universal male assignment for women whose behavior they do not understand. You will be a psycho, you will get dismissed and, worse yet, you will not get to savor any more of that good tasty lovin'.

- You have no time to assess *his* psychodom. This is very important. These are not the olden days when June Cleaver could bang out a quickie in the laundry room with the milkman and not be afraid he'd be lurking in her azaleas for the next three months alternately weeping and tapping on the kitchen window with an empty milk bottle. You do not want to let a strange guy into your home, let alone your body, without vetting him first. Let's be clear. Your body is a temple. A nice, clean, hot, curvy temple, and none shall pass without proper clearance.

All right, enough with the lecture. You're not listening anyway. We are incapable of heeding the advice of others when it comes to potentially humiliating situations. We can't help it. It's how we're wired. As you march off toward inevitable degradation, just remember to protect your eyes and soft parts. The best offense is a good defense. Or more apropos: when engaged in offense, remember your defense.

I Am the Captain of
My Ship

or
Why Won't He Call Me?
Why? Why? Why? Why?

I think if you want to arrive at the end of your life fat, happy, and satisfied, you have to have racked up a certain number of hours of humiliation, poor judgment, and abject regret.

I don't know how many hours that is, but I wish I did, because then I'd know whether I was ahead or behind my quota. If I was ahead, I could just stop making mistakes right away and get the rest of it right from here on out. If I was behind, I could go do something awful like try to throw out the first pitch at a Dodger game or play in a pro-am golf tournament or do avant-garde theater, and get all the rest of my hours in at once. I like to be efficient.

I happen to think I'm ahead, mainly because of a couple of guys I dated when I was younger. It's one thing entirely to fool around or have a fling with a guy who later turns out to be a waste of carbon; it's another thing entirely to spend months or even years with the donkey. There's a point at which you say to yourself, *Self, this guy is a donkey. Why am I still here? I should pack up my Redd Foxx album collection and my saltwater fish tank and get the hell out.* Why don't you listen to yourself at that point? No, you think, *Self doesn't know what the hell she's talking about. Self is an idiot. She's just a disembodied voice in my head. What does she know?* And you continue hanging out with the donkey, even though he doesn't treat you very nicely, never defends you when his housemates make fun of you, and is always borrowing money for CornNuts.

I think the fact that the guy is a donkey is usually much more apparent than we want to acknowledge when we first start hanging out with the donkey. There are signs; there are *always* signs. He's incredibly attentive before you start fooling around; afterwards he's got to get up early to do "some charcoal sketches." He calls you every day for a week, and then suddenly disappears into the ether; when you see him again he says he was *"crazy* busy, man." You see him with a girl that he claims is his sister, even though she seems to have been born in another country, somewhere on the Indian subcontinent. But no, you keep talking to this guy, and hanging out at his house, and doing his homework for him. *Wake up,* self says. *He is a donkey.* And you ignore self until many years later when you come across some old e-mail he wrote you, asking for money and extolling the virtues of ranch-flavored CornNuts, and in your head, you see a large, braying *burro*.

There are ways to save yourself. Like the Navy Seals say, always allow for an exit strategy.[55] There were any number of points along the track with my donkeys where I could've jumped, but I didn't. Which is why if I ever find out how many hours of humiliation I have left to rack up, I'm sure I'll find I'm very close to done.

The call

You want the short answer? You shouldn't call. If you worry that you should, you shouldn't. Usually, if we're worried about calling, it's because we've already called once, or maybe even twice or three times, and he hasn't called back, and we're starting to sound autistic on his answering machine, saying the same things over and over again and asking him to call, each time trying harder to sound casual and failing on a grander and grander scale. I hate to say that not calling gives you the upper hand, but it does. This is why guys don't call, because they are terrified of being humiliated, and thus are loath to relinquish the upper hand by calling and putting the ball in your court. Exercise restraint. If you do, and he still pursues, and sets you at ease that he's cool, likes you, and doesn't need to

~AISHA TYLER~

55. I don't know if they actually say that but it seems like something they would approve of.

borrow any money, you can go to a more normalized calling schedule. This is not about playing games or being some kind of manipulative ice queen. It's about having control over your own life. Look at those days in between calls as an opportunity to figure out how many cards this guy's actually got in his deck.

If, on the other hand, you don't care about who has the upper hand, or if you're just too smitten to give a damn, go ahead. It won't kill you. Just no screaming, crying, or pleading on tape. That always comes back to bite you.

Mr. Freaknasty

A little perversion is okay. What healthy girl doesn't like a spanking once in a while? But what if a fun night of experimentation suddenly turns your backdoor man into a weeping infant, or a demanding lout who's pulling your hair so hard he's removing highlights? This is another indication that you should throw the donkey out with the bathwater immediately. If he is comfortable being this nasty now, think about what he's going to feel comfortable with in a few years! Protect your backside from excessive and unnecessary whuppings and other distasteful activities. Disengage now. You want to avoid having to call an ex-boyfriend for a little strong-arm sex creep exorcism. That's just two donkeys in your life.

Again, if you are all into the corporal punishment, more power to you. Just don't suffer through it and then secretly wish he was hit by a tsunami. That is very ineffectual. Tsunamis are quite, quite rare.

There's the door

You have done the extraordinary, the unheard of, the highly improbable. You have deduced that the donkey is a donkey early enough in the game to slap him on his hindquarters and send him on his way. Maybe on a first or second date even. Pat yourself on the back—you're a better girl than I. What do you do now? He seems to want to stay, if only because he saw you had bologna slices in your fridge. You want him to go, so you can get a good night's sleep, shower thoroughly, and begin the long slow process of recovery. But the sack of inert human flesh has the audacity to snore right in front of you as you're trying to spread out across the bed and make your bed angels (you know, like in the snow, only with sheets). You want nothing more than for him to leave, and take his underpants off the ceiling light as he does. In this case, a little subterfuge goes a long way.

I'm not saying you should turn into a big fat liar. But sometimes you have to pad the truth a little to save yourself from further mortification down the line. These are tried and true strategies that have worked for millions over the eons; you no doubt have already encountered one of them coming out of the lyin' ass piehole of a guy. Time to turn the tables.

1. **The Early Meeting:** "I have to be up early for a meeting and I don't want to disturb you when I get up to shower and douche."

2. **The I Can't Sleep with Other People in the Bed:** "I have this awful condition. I sleep-box. It's like sleepwalking only I beat the shit out of whoever's lying next to me."

3. **The This Is All Happening So Fast!:** "Now that we have made the love, I need to know how you really feel about me. *What does this all mean? What? What? What!?*"

4. **The Coups de Grace:**
    i. "I'm pregnant, and even though we only just slept together, I think it's yours. I can feel it. I can sense these things. I'm psychic."
    ii. "I'm married and I think I hear his keys in the front-door lock. Don't worry, though. His gun is all the way at the other end of the house. You have at least four minutes."
    iii. "Even though we've only known each other for ten days, I think I love you." Accompany this with a white-knuckle deathgrip on his extremities and a quavering lip for effect.[56]

---

56. This one must be used very gingerly and with great prudence, in case you have a sentimental fool on your hands who feels exactly the same way. That could lead to a *very* sticky extraction.

5. **When All Else Fails—The Cry:** Feel free to put your own personal spin on this one. This is your time to shine. Vamp it up!

Goodnight, nurse!

Let's say the alarm never goes off. You've been seeing that unassuming smoothie jockey from your gym. He's well-read, likes both foreign films and kickass blockbusters, can make a mean swordfish, and does naughty things that make you scream so loud the ghost of your dead grandmother crossed over to tell you to keep it down. Keep an ear to the ground, but it sounds like you may have a keeper. If none of your triggers are being pulled, wipe your brow and thank your lucky stars.

But what if, after a few months, you start to get a prickly feeling on the back of your neck, like you're falling really fast, and you realize that it's because the old sweetie has become vapors, and a new, more donkeylike guy has taken his place, like some kind of horrible body-snatching jackass? There's still time to ditch him and save yourself a few humiliation man hours. Let's find out what Sun Tzu says one more time. That guy lived a long time ago, but he sure was smart!

Sun Tzu said: When a chieftain is fighting in his own territory, it is dispersive ground. When he has penetrated into hostile territory, it is facile ground. Ground the possession of which imports great advantage to either side, is contentious ground. On dispersive ground, therefore, fight not. On facile ground, halt not. On contentious ground, attack not. On contentious ground, I would hurry up my rear.

I don't quite know what this means, because the guy who translated this from the original Chinese thought he had to get really fancy with this passage. But I have an idea. If applied to cutting off your festering limb of a guy before the gangrene reaches internal organs, it means, on your own territory, be calm and direct, tell him it's over, and that he needs to go as soon as possible. Packing up his stuff beforehand, or telling him right before he has to leave for work can help hasten his departure, with minimum drama for you. On neutral territory, you can drop the bomb and get the hell out yourself. Again, be blunt and direct. No one likes a bullshitter. On his territory, hurry up your rear. I think that's pretty self-explanatory, no?

Brave New World

or
I Am Lazy and
I Like to Party

So I'm in a hotel room in Charlotte, North Carolina. A lovely little city, much more cosmopolitan than you would think. In-house sushi chefs at the supermarkets, fabulous gay men manning the MAC counter down at the Belk (which is a fancy southern way of saying Macy's). However, you'd never know it from my surroundings. I have, somehow, ended up in quite the armpit of a hotel room. It's in an acceptable enough hotel, which is why I agreed to check into it in the first place. However, I must have ended up in the room where the murders took place,[57] because the whole thing reeks of camphor, that waxy substance that coroners smudge on their upper lip to mask the smell of

---

57. Every hotel has a room where the murders took place. It's a rule, like not having a thirteenth floor or charging fifty dollars for two boiled eggs and a pot of coffee.

rotting flesh. The smell is eye-wateringly overwhelming the minute I walk in the door; after twenty minutes I start looking under the bed for telltale bloodstains or a severed hand. In the middle of the night I get up and cover the bed with the extra sheets from the closet, worried about disturbing DNA evidence, or worse, getting bits of microscopic human goo on my forearms while I sleep.

By the next morning, I have lost all sense of smell and taste, and am slumped over in the bed, positive that a dying man writhed on the bedspread in the throes of death only hours before I checked in. I flick on the television, too woozy to move, and vow (in my head) to get up in just a few minutes, call the police, and check into a different hotel room. Not necessarily in that order. *Just a few minutes*, I mumble, as drool falls slowly from my camphor-deadened tongue. *I'll watch television for a few minutes and then some heads are gonna roll!*

Through no fault of my own, *The View* is on. I didn't choose it, it just shows up on the television. Because I am dying a slow, suffocating death, I cannot lift my hand to change the channel. So I watch. And I ponder.

I cannot decide how I feel about *The View*. On the one hand, it is supposed to be an empowering show, a frank conversation between "girlfriends" about what "girlfriends" really think about. They talk frankly about sex (kinda), pillory sexist cultural pressures (sorta), and deconstruct cutting edge political themes (in a way). It's a mass media show, so they can't be *too* sassy. Plus, Barbara Walters is there, keeping an eye on things, making sure the kibitzing keeps a PG-65 rating so the cashmered old ladies won't cough up their fiber cereal. She's like a human governor, keeping the conversation at a safe and sane forty miles an hour.

Tellingly, the young ones keep jumping ship. First, Debbie Matenopulos, who, I have to say, I was glad to see go, because I certainly didn't need her representing my generation. To me, she was a finger in the eye of conversation, queen of the malaprop, and, from what I could tell, never met a mispronunciation she didn't like. I would gradually deflate as I watched her bungle in the jungle, thinking "Gee, if that was the best they could find, maybe my generation *is* poorly informed and superficial. Now that I think about it, I *do* feel kind of dumb and out of touch with public affairs." She was a daily blow to my self-image.

They finally wised up and replaced Debbie with Lisa Ling, who I liked infinitely better. She was smart and beautiful, and before she was on *The View*, she used to do the news. Granted, it was for Channel One, and only seen in high school homerooms when the regular teacher was out sick and the substitute had given up on getting the kids to do any actual work, but it was a heck of a lot more reportage than Joy Behar had ever done. She was outspoken and serious and only occasionally did her fashion choices upset or offend, as opposed to the rest of the ladies, who regularly looked like a publicity photo for an early episode of *Knots Landing*. Lisa was cool. She stuck it out for a while, too, holding fast the ramparts of youth against the onslaught of four women for whom *attitude* meant cackling "You go, girl!" while snapping their fingers like some kind of cartoon Little Richard. And let me say that the real Little Richard is already pretty cartoony.

Soon enough, however, Lisa had to jump ship as well. Why? Why was she leaving all of us relative tykes without a representative on the venerable *View* board? It was a cushy job on a hit show and it didn't seem like much work. All she had to do was grill celebrity guests with an occasional question from those big blue index cards and pretend to find the guy who explained how to make hair conditioner out of mayonnaise for just pennies a treatment riveting. Why'd she bail?

I have a theory. It's because the show isn't what it claims to be. It isn't that radical, it isn't that modern, it isn't that conflict-driven, and the viewpoints aren't really that diverse. It's like a live-action *Cosmopolitan:* for all of its professed radical modernism, G-spot diagrams, and Kama Sutra quizzes, the Wizard of Oz behind the curtain is a pleasant septuagenarian.

Still, the show is supposed to be an open, bluntly honest conversation between women with various viewpoints. (I do wonder why no one ever has an open, honest conversation about the fact that Star Jones' hairstyle changes more times in a week than the NASDAQ ticker. She must spend every minute she's not on the show or shilling Payless shoes in a stylist's chair. It's quite impressive, in a peculiar way.) So why am I yawning and slumping deeper into that haunted bed? Why aren't I bolt upright, riveted by the ribaldry and soul-baring commentary? I squint and try to concentrate harder. The tiny candle I have lit to combat the chemical smell strains to overpower its surroundings, like a tiny superhero fighting a much larger alien invader with heat vision and death-ray eyes.

I remember that, a few years ago, when *The View* was young, Meredith Viera made a decision not to color her hair anymore. She's getting older, and naturally going gray—most Americans in this era of Botox and microliposuction don't realize this, but older people's hair gets gray, James Woods and Regis Philbin notwithstanding—and she had decided not to succumb to the pressures of popular culture to stay young-looking. If men could go gray gracefully, then so could she, goddammit! She announced it on the show with plucky hope, a wild-eyed protest against the juggernaut of the beauty machine. The other girls in the coffee klatsch pluckily applauded her, as did the plucky studio audience. *You go, girl! Show them how it's done! Embrace the silver crone within!* It was a veritable maelstrom of pluck as Meredith bravely set off on her path to beauty righteousness.

And then it all went horribly awry. She started getting letters. Horrible, venomous, eviscerating letters. From *other women.* I don't know where these women live, or who they are, or how they managed to put pen to paper and construct whole sentences, but these women were mad. Furious, even. *"How dare you let yourself go?"*[58] *"You owe it to your husband to look as beautiful as you can at all times!"*[59] *"It's laziness, pure laziness."*[60] *"You go color your hair this minute, and get some highlights too. You're a mess!"*[61] Where are we? I thought. No, *when* are we?

Aha! I exulted, in my junky hotel room (we're back to the present). *That's it! The show appeals to women who want to feel radical but aren't really.* It's one thing to make a face mask out of olive oil and sea salt, and another thing altogether to throw out fifty years of social norms and start really thinking differently. And the ladies of *The View* know that. So as modern as they'd like to think they are, in the end they still feel uncomfortable about flouting the norm, because the people who watch the show certainly aren't about to start doing anything so wild and crazy as to ask a guy on a date, admit they enjoy sex, or (gasp!) let their natural hair color grow in.

I'm starting to feel like a genius. I sit up in bed, feeling smug. I look around but there's no one to share my self-satisfaction with, so I share it with the ghost of the guy

58. These are not actual quotes, but approximate paraphrases based on my recollection of the show. At the time I watched it I didn't know I was going to include it in the book. Hell, I didn't even know I was going to write a book. Those were halcyon days.
59. *Ibid.*
60. *Ibid.*
61. Yup, *ibid.*

who died there. "I've got it. This show sucks because it's got no *balls*." The ghost doesn't respond. I figure he's just basking in the brilliance of my deduction. I sink back among the pillows, now mildly interested in what comes next, if only because I hope it will reinforce my slowly forming testicular theory.

Aforementioned theory gets its validation when one of the ladies pulls out a copy of the magazine *Jane* and began flipping through it. Let me say here quickly that I love *Jane*. It is a truly modern women's magazine, full of dry wit, dirty jokes, ill-behaved women, and one-night stand how-tos. Other magazines pretend to be modern but shoot themselves in the literary foot every time they run a four-page article on mascara or follow some made-up guy through a week's worth of his "dating misadventures." *Jane* is the real deal. Even I am occasionally scandalized by its hubris. And honey, I ain't scandalized by much. I can have a two-hour conversation with a room full of boys about bodily functions and come out on top.

The first thing I fall in love with is the spine of the magazine, which says, *I am lazy and I like to party.* I immediately feel a deep emotional connection with each and every girl working at this magazine, and vow to call them all and tell them how cool they are, if I live after twenty-four hours in this Bunsen burner of a room. The cover has Pamela Anderson on it (I reserve comment), which makes me feel as if I won't call *all* of them, only some (although now I'm not sure which ones). They quickly scrabble forward to the item of interest: a spread inside called "Pages and Pages of Naked Guys for No Good Reason." At this point I am completely vertical, riveted. This sounds like my kind of feature. I have felt for quite a while that women's magazines don't do enough to narrow the gap between themselves and the abject objectification of women in such bald, snarky lifestyle publications as *FHM* and *Stuff*. Why is it that they can illustrate a feature on the importance of regular auto maintenance with three half-naked girls dressed up like Manny, Moe, and Jack (the Pep Boys), but the most we get is some blue-eyed soap opera look-alike mooning balefully at us from an article on difficult breakups? I want to see some skin! And finally, it seems, *Jane* has heard my many silent, telepathic pleas to the cosmos. I make a mental note to rush out and get a copy of the issue of *Jane* as soon as I muster the will to shamble out of the tomb room. I am quite, quite pleased.

My smile takes an instant nosedive when the women begin blaspheming about how this gorgeous gem of a feature, this photographic essay born of divine inspiration, is *yucky*. Behar even has the nerve to say, "Who would want to see that?" I almost faint dead away. Thank god I'm already in bed.

What is it about our sexuality that makes us feel constantly compelled to deny it? Why is it that we can't admit being attracted to men, objectifying them, even feeling sexually predatory toward them? Whenever you see a woman fawning over a man on television, she's swooning, she's fanning, she's about to faint dead away like Scarlett O'Hara after hearing that Hattie McDaniel had moved out, started her own record company, become filthy rich, and bought a compound in the Hamptons. Our sexual fantasies, when expressed on television, are romantic ones, involving candlelight, champagne, massages, and lots of hugging with the lights out. Not that all of that stuff isn't great stuff—hugging is super!—but we don't get to have any other kinds of fantasies, ones where we pick out a guy based solely on his looks, or his abs, or his ass, or the pheromone mushroom cloud he throws up when he walks through a room. Why? Because you would seem slutty and indiscriminate to your friends. Slutty *and* indiscriminate. Woof. That's a combo. Why don't guys get the slutty/indiscriminate label? Because it doesn't sell beer. And, as we all know, beer is the fulcrum around which the entire American economy rotates; wobbling a bit because it's two-thirds into a twelve pack and it hasn't eaten lunch yet.

Every beer commercial is about boobies. Sooner or later, at some point in the thirty seconds, you're going to see a rack. Or three. A big, heaving, well-oiled rack, jiggling away in some fantasy nightclub where all the girls are hot and hyperstacked and all the guys are homely and google-eyed at their good fortune. In this killer fantasy world, there are half-naked waitresses and halter-topped damsels in distress and gorgeous twins caught inexplicably in the line of fire of a lawn sprinkler with no choice but to whip their voluminous hair from left to right to avoid the water's deadly spray and swimwear models enraged over their best friend's bullheaded belief that beer tastes great when everyone knows it's less filling and women engaged in highly critical contract negotiations involving a large bed and a lot of feather pillows. And everywhere, the racks heave. Heaving breasts here, jiggling boobulation there, here a boob, there a boob, everywhere a boob-boob. I'm surprised Anheuser-Busch (ironic name, no?) hasn't come out with a beer simply called Booby Beer. Or perhaps Boobrau. Or Rackenheiser. Or Pilsner DD. Cold filtered through a bra for that fresh boob taste.

Beer sales have been flat in recent years, which explains the explosion of soda-like malt liquor treats that have been proliferating around town like Zima's second coming. The Smirnoff Ices and the Mike's Hard Lemonades and the other assorted new-millennium wine coolers. That's what they all are, wine coolers. When I was a kid, we drank Ciscos, and now people drink Skyy Blue. I am always looking around for Bartles & Jaymes to come jumping out from behind a bush—or Busch—in one of these ads and screech, Gomer Pyle–style, "Surprise, surprise, surprise! We was here all along! We know the old coolers were too girly, but we done figgered it out and now we gotcha hooked! You kin tell yer friends it tastes just like a gin in tonic but we both know you're drinking a nice, delicious, lemony wine cooler! And thank you for yer support!"

By contrast, here is an alcohol advertisement directed specifically at women. A bunch of lovely ladies sit together on a beachside patio, demure flowered skirts and cotton–merino cardigans gathered properly around their legs, and watch as their bumbling gang of chosen ones scrabble to build a sand castle in exchange for a glass of some melonberry flavored "wine." There's lots of chuckling and tittering and other mild demonstrations of amusement, because truthfully, how excited can you get about melonberry *anything*? Why don't they just add a couple of fifths of Popov vodka to a garbage can full of Hi-C and call it a day? So the guys huff and puff and build some huge monstrosity of a sand thing, just to get an extra glass of the boozy Hi-C, and the women practically high-five each other because their men are all down on the beach building a meaningless structure out of sand instead of being up on the patio showing off their well-oiled ab muscles or grilling up some big ol' steaks for the ladies or I don't know, arguing over who's going to get the big room in the beach house rental later on when it's time for *making ze love*.

If I haven't made my point, it's that we young women are getting robbed. The television shows that claim to represent us are about as current as the stack of *Reader's Digests* in your OB/GYN's waiting room. Hell, we don't even get any gratuitous sex in our booze commercials. If you can't be pandered to where alcohol is concerned, what justice is there in the world?

Jane, I think, is one of the few truly authentic postmodern voices for girls. In that same issue, there was an article entitled "The First-Ever Shame-Free Girls' Guide to One-Night Stands." It was full of happy little instructions, useful things to remember, like how to deal with an unexpected in-bed bladder disaster; how to surreptitiously inspect your temporary lover for, ahem, sores of various and sundry kinds; and how to throw him out on his coccyx after you've had your way with him. It used the word *slutty* in reference to guys repeatedly, and actually recommended that you toss the guy out if he can't perform rather than try to help him get his colonel to stand at attention. The exact phrase the article used was "screw that noise," which I suspect is derived from the phrase "fuck that noise," a phrase that my friends and I sprinkled rather liberally throughout our conversation during the eighth and ninth grades, applying it with equal fervor to situations both positive and negative.[62] We just liked saying it.

The article was genius on about seventeen levels, but

62. As in: you're standing in the street with a group of friends and someone comes up to you and tells you that it's going to cost ten bucks to get into a keg party. You respond, "Fuck that noise. If we all put our ten bucks together

the level I liked most was that you couldn't quite tell if it was serious or not. It was hilarious, and at the same time imparted some important information, including safe-sex suggestions and how to avoid being caught in an unsafe situation with a possible predator. There was an admonition not to have unprotected oral sex, followed by the post–broken condom contingency plan of "jumping up and down and queefing a lot" (I can be pretty sure, without being a doctor or anything, that that doesn't work). So, was it a comedy piece or an advice article? Modern or postmodern? Art or commerce?

I mean really, who cares? That magazine is just cool.

This is why the *Jane* incident on *The View* was so . . . I dunno, disheartening. Because, finally, a publication expressed some of what we are really thinking and feeling—that we are sexual beings, with needs and desires and the capacity for superficiality and wanton sex. And that sometimes it's okay to look at a guy's ass (okay, most of the time), and that it doesn't need to be couched in the guise of romanticism or giggled away in a cloud of self-consciousness, but can be bloodlessly presented as the objectification it really

---

we could buy our own keg and put it in the trunk of your car." Or you're at a friend's house drinking (what else? a wine cooler) and your friend says that the boy you like is in the living room playing quarters. "Fuck this noise!" you exclaim, pounding your cooler, tossing the bottle into the sink and skipping into the living room like a hopscotch champ. Universally applicable, verbally effective. It's a gem of a phrase.

is, an objectification that all people engage in, male and female because, for chrissake, we're *animals*, and all these old broads pooh-poohed it. Ugh. Brave New World, indeed.

The vanguard is a lonely place, my friend. A lonely, camphor-scented place.

Martha Stewart
on Crack

It's Saturday afternoon, and there's fat all over my computer keys. My hair smells like meat, my shirt is splattered with lamb juices, and my fingers are glistening with duck fat. Duck fat.

I have been cooking all morning, trying to make a French casserole called *cassoulet*. I have had *cassoulet* just once in my entire life, in a little bistro in Toronto. But it was incredible. So incredible that I have been trying to repeat the experience ever since. Far be it from me to do my taxes or pay my bills, or maybe wash my birdpoop-encrusted car, no, those things are mundane, unimportant. I am in dogged, breathless, one-minded pursuit of a good *cassoulet*.

If you've never had *cassoulet*, it's a bean and meat concoction that has so many varieties of meat products in it—

bacon, lamb, pork, duck, lamb sausage, pork sausage, and if you like (and I don't), pig's feet—that I imagine the entire neighborhood is wondering where the slaughterhouse fire is. The cloud of aromatic meat smoke is so large and overpowering I'm convinced Jacques Pepin is going to materialize at my front door any minute and show me just the right way to bone a mallard.

I like to cook. In fact, I love it. I cook all the time. In fact, I do almost all the cooking in my house. If I'm home, I'd rather make something from scratch than order in or crack a can. Not that I won't eat something out of a can, or even a frozen pizza under the right circumstances (those circumstances being either drunk, hungover, or minutes before the apocalypse), but I prefer home-cooked food. In fact, I'm obsessed with it (I'm also clearly obsessed with the phrase "in fact").

In my life, I have made many, many things from scratch. Many of these things could have been made from a mix or, better yet, purchased easily and cheaply from a corner store without breaking a sweat or starting a grease fire. Somehow, I insist on doing things the hard way. I have made pancakes and chocolate mousse and frosting. I have smoked a turkey and made yogurt and ice cream and bread and pasta, knowing full well that those things were waiting for me down at the supermarket like fat little luscious Christmas presents, just waiting to be taken home for one dollar and ninety-nine cents or less. I have baked Italian wedding cookies and made saltwater taffy and have, on quite a few occasions, been, I believe, the only black girl in the world to bake challah for the Jewish sabbath. I have tried my hand at pie crusts and potato chips, puff pastry and even cheese. (Good lord, *cheese!* Why would I do that?) I have, not once, but multiple times, brewed my own beer. I even contemplated making my own wine, never bothering to consider how much wine was to be had for the price of the six or seven bottles of marginally drinkable nectar I would have been able to produce in my closet. That's right, my closet. I will sell no wine before its time—to move all my winter boots into storage.

I like to think I do all this because I'm a purist, committed to understanding the origins of things and the satisfaction that comes from having handcrafted something from scratch. But the truth is that most of the time it's more work than it's worth. I could have just gone to the store and bought a bag of ravioli, rather than getting up at five in the morning to roll the pasta, make the filling, and stack them meticulously on a floured cookie sheet, only to have them explode like tiny land mines in boiling water, making a kind of cheesy, curdy, eggy, water soup, and sending me and my ravenous, and by this time quite enraged, houseguests scampering to the nearest Pizza Hut. Why don't I let the whole scratch cooking thing go? What makes me hold on to such an arcane experience? Why would a postmodern girl make her *own ravioli* for chrissake?

Because people who cook are cool. They're mysterious

and mathematical and people admire them. For some reason, takeout and frozen foods and instant pudding have rendered cooking as mystical as quantum physics. Fewer and fewer people understand how it works, or even that it can be done by any one other than Martha Stewart or that plump guy with the clogs on the cooking channel. Plain and simple, scratch cooks are up there with brain surgeons and NASCAR drivers when it comes to "Man, I wish I knew how to do that" activities. You bring a bag of homemade cookies to the beach, or make your best friend's birthday cake, and people will coo "You *made* that?" in a way that they never do for people who do mundane things like fix cars or birth babies. You will be a Nobel Prize winner, a computer programmer, a rock star.

I'm not advocating that you become some kind of domestic obsessive, puttering around your kitchen stringing up ducks by their necks and canning rhubarb. (Who the hell eats rhubarb? Who even knows what it is? Is it a vegetable? A fruit? Red celery? No one knows but three or four zaftig ladies at roadside diners in the middle of the country, and they're not telling you *nothin'*.) I *am* saying that being able to cook is a cool thing to do. We are past the time when not cooking was some kind of political statement, a rejection of the old gender expectations, and a declaration of one's independence. Fortunately, most of us didn't even have to suffer through it, as it was before our time. But the seventies and eighties were ripe for the obvious feminist statement, the overt proclamations and strident cheek that arises when a social movement gets co-opted by Madison Avenue. The girls who came before us had to suffer through the awful Virginia Slims campaign ("You've come a long way, baby," and that means you can get cancer like the boys now, only from fashionably slim cigarettes rather than the big, fat, clunky masculine ones) and blunt force films like *Baby Boom* and *Working Girl* (hey! women are smart! they can do stuff! and in Pro Keds and bangs that could cut a man in half, no less!) and layouts in *Vogue* that told them they were free to do what they wanted and when, as long as they had on a sensationally slim pencil skirt.

And then there was that awful perfume ad. I was just a pup, a wee bun, but I remember it vividly, because the jingle was so invasive, so cancerously catchy that, even to this day I can sing it back to you word for word. I think I must have been about three years old, but even then, I knew that women can "bring home the bacon, fry it up in the pan, and never let you forget you're a man," all the while smelling like a cross between baby oil and my grandmother's living-room couch. That commercial was meant to be some kind of dramatic, libertine stab at "the establishment," a brazen declaration of female independence, a new world perfume manifesto. Instead, it was the creepiest, kookiest exercise in the blatantly obvious ever perpetuated by an advertising firm. The reason we don't see that kind of stuff on television now? Because we already know that stuff. We know we can have bacon and fry it and get some lovin' while we're at it. Right? We post-modern girls are past it.

Right?

I don't trust a woman who says she doesn't cook. I know this is a decidedly nonmodern, arcane, flowered apron and "where's the Beaver?" kind of attitude, but hang in there with me. You can say you don't *like* to cook, or you don't have time to cook, or you've tried to cook several times but it always ends up burned and with the faint flavor of human fingertip. But what I can't stand is when women wave their hands dismissively and say, "Oh, I don't cook." The implication is greater than their ten-second dismissal. What they're really saying is "I don't cook, because cooking is for grandmothers and television weathermen and Filipino mail-order brides. I am a modern woman, and modern women are not chained to their stove. I am demonstrating just how modern and fabulous and unencumbered by gender stereotypes I am by consisting on a diet of Chin Chin Chinese Chicken Salads and Diet Coke. Sure, I'm sallow and exhausted and my bones have the integrity of a Wiffleball, but I am so, incredibly, unbelievably *liberated*."

A woman who cooks is the sexiest thing in the world. I know this, because a guy who cooks is the sexiest thing in the world. If you meet a guy who offers to cook for you and then actually *does it*, and what he slides in front of you doesn't make you want to renounce your U.S. citizenship, then keep that guy around. I'm not saying marry him, but make sure you can call on him on a regular basis, either for sex or as a great cosmic pheromone ball to help get you sex from someone else. Guys who can cook ooze sexy. They are so in touch with their masculinity that they think nothing of owning a set of matching mixing bowls or making a *mirepoix*. A guy like that is going to be a fireball in bed. He has no fear of the feminine. (Unless he's gay, and then he may have some mild discomfort with the feminine. But at the very least you'll have a great new best friend who can cook.)

And I hate to say this—in fact, my face is contorting a little bit just from thinking it, because I know you're going to throw up your hands and chuck the book across the room again, yelling "What is the deal with this chick? I'm being lectured by the young, black Julia Child!" I just hope you bought this thing in hardback—the spines are much better able to withstand repeated drywall collisions—but the fastest way to a guy's heart is through his stomach. Hold it! No chucking yet! The fastest way to a guy's heart is through his stomach, not because once you've cooked for him he can imagine you in his kitchen, barefoot and sweaty, stirring a pot of meat pieces, your heaving bosom dusted with flour and your bottom peeking out of the back of a French maid's outfit (although that image could work for quite a few men, and some women as well, I imagine). It's because a confident, modern, independent girl who cooks is cool enough not to worry about how cool she is. She isn't worried about what kind of precedent she's setting or what gender role she's locking into or whether she can persuade some guy to like her by making him prime rib instead of just being her fabulous, scintillating self. She's just doing her thing, and her thing includes making some incredible meal he's never had before, not because she's expected to, but because she *can*.

You don't have to be a nutjob like me, trying to turn cane juice into sugar or handcraft your own pats of butter. You can cook any way you like. It can be as simple as a salad or pasta or eggs, or you can try to whip up something more complex (just not that agglomeration of ramen noodles, canned chili, and cheddar cheese that you try to convince your friends is stir fry—that's just wrong). Only eating food that other people make, without knowing what went into it, is dangerous. Just look at what happened to Violet Beauregarde when she chewed Willy Wonka's gum. *She* turned into a giant blueberry.

I cook. I cook every chance I get. I love to eat, and so I love to cook. I don't always have the time but, whenever I get an evening at home, I make something from scratch. It's therapy for me. I get to relax, slow down, think, and, at the end, I get to eat something! Oh, man, everybody wins.

Stay on the Path

or

How Not to Get
Addickted

I feel adventurous. Let's go on a little trip back to the eighth grade. No, you say? The eighth grade was torture, pure emotional duress packed into eight periods and homeroom, the beginning of the end of your happy, golden, preteen view of the world and your place in it? Well, it was for me, too. It was for *everybody*, except for that one blond girl who already had boobs and perfect teeth and seemed to have a zillion friends, and a couple of guys with long hair and bad skin who looked like losers on the outside but couldn't really give a fuck what anyone thought of them and so were the happiest thirteen-year-olds on the planet.

Sorry, but I insist. We are going back to the eighth grade. It's important. The eighth grade is when most of us started thinking about sex (not you, you early-adopting, overly mature, prepubescent Mrs. Robinson). At least it was in my day. Nowadays, nine-year-olds are running backroom mah-jongg operations and playing the horses, so I have no idea. But while I had noticed boys much earlier, it was in the eighth grade that I had my first kiss, my first grope, and all of the attendant angst and self-doubt that went along with it.

Thank god that was a long time ago. The problem is that the way we thought then and the way we think now hasn't changed that much. Not much at all. We have such a hypersexual society now, every song, every video, every magazine cover practically drips sex all over your supermarket cart, dampening your carton of eggs and making your low-fat frozen yogurt container sticky. Almost every one of these images is female, inviting you in, staring you down, pouting as if to say "I'm naughty and I need to be punished!" One would think this meant that we are finally able to be overtly sexual in a strong way, that women's sexuality was finally on a par with men's. But no. Now, as much as ever, women are branded as sluts for having active sex lives, while no one bats an eye at the man-whores running around, spreading cold sores like Johnny Appleseed.

Look at a woman like Jennifer Lopez, who's only been married twice, fergawdsakes. She's certainly no Larry King or James Woods. Yet the fact that she's been through two divorces is the longest-running joke in late night television. And people express all kinds of disdain for a woman who, before our very eyes, has built a multimedia empire with her bare hands. Anyone, male or female, who worked hard enough to do what she has would have lost a couple of spouses along the way. It's par for the course—long hours, fierce devotion to career, one-mindedness to the exclusion of all else equals relationship deflating like a high-altitude cake. When a guy spends all his time building a career, to the detriment of his marriage, we hardly take notice. But a woman does it and she's malice personified, a four-headed hydra in Armani. It's really, really lame. I'm not saying that all women should run out and do what Lopez did; for the first thing, there's only one P. Diddy to go around.[63]

We are constantly applying the pall of sluttiness to women who are, in reality, quite chaste. Britney Spears is a perfect example. Yes, her stage act trades on sexuality, but what pop star's doesn't? That's the price of entry nowadays. If you aren't engaged in a simulated (or not so simulated) strip show every time you appear on television you're dismissed as irrelevant. People want to call Britney slutty, but we all know she's only been with one guy in her whole life. *Everyone* knows that. Yet she's a hypersexualized young woman, and that makes everyone uncomfortable. So we dismiss her, diminish her, devalue her by calling her *slutty*. No matter that she's a multiplatinum artist responsible for millions of dollars in album sales. Compare her to an artist like D'Angelo, who did an

63. I'm sure he would agree.

entire video completely naked, the camera frame continually dipping precipitously close to the water line.[64] That video wasn't suggestive. There was no subtle implication of any kind whatsoever. The dude was *naked*. You can't get a more blunt statement than that. Now D's sold a lot of albums, for sure, but (sadly) not nearly as many as Britney. No one's calling *him* slutty. Why is it that we respect the slutty guy and not the slutty girl? We even go so far, some of us women, as to be attracted to the slutty guy, knowing full well he's a whore who won't remember our name in the morning and will tell stories about us to his friends, most of which won't be true, and the parts that are true shouldn't be spoken outside a confessional or a deathbed. We actually think we'll get in bed with this guy and change his mind, that we'll be the girl to make him lay down his sleaze flag and turn to a life of devotion. Trust me; it doesn't work that way. Einstein proved it in a theorem somewhere: the "slutty guys cannot be magically converted into nice ones through sex = MC^2" theorem.

If you want to sleep with the slutty guy knowing full well he's a slut and that he probably picked up a few tricks along the way from which you might benefit, go ahead. If your intention is to have a good time, forget his name in the morning, and tell stories about *him* to *your* friends,

64. Not that I'm complaining. I would actually like to take this opportunity to personally thank D'Angelo for the video for "How Does It Feel," which has brought me and countless others an immeasurable amount of deep, soul-buoying joy. Man, that dude's got abs!

all of which will be true but far too explicit even for a group of guys, then fine. Just know that going in, and then *be cool.*

Because this is one of the biggest mistakes we make with guys when we're trying to hit it and quit it. We're *not cool.* We make doe eyes at him across the bar. We giggle and point with our friends from the table in the corner. We stumble out of the club, buzzed in full view of everyone, tell our life story to him in the car on the way to his place, ask about girls in pictures, ask about his parents, ask about who he slept with last, about who he's sleeping with now, ask, ask, ask. We're overly friendly when we see him next, looking for assurance that we're the special one, the different one, the life-changer. The fact is, nothing's special or life-changing about a one-night stand. Nothing. You go home with someone on a first date, you better get yours, get out, and get on with your life before you have to have a sober conversation with the guy in the light of day. Before shame and panic forces you into finding a relationship that *isn't there in the first place.*

Sex is not love. This is the single greatest mistake young women (and men) make in their lives. Sex. Is. Not. Love. Somehow, some grand cosmic joke has made women believe that letting a guy into their beds means letting them into our lives. We sleep with some dude we found mildly loathsome when first meeting him, have what turns out to be whiplash sex, then suddenly conjure up mental tableau of our three bedroom, two bath split-level ranch in the country with the koi pond and the sandstone kitchen flooring. Disabuse yourself of this. It is a path of destruction.

Sex leads to affection. Affection leads to attachment. Attachment leads to resentment. Resentment leads to hate. Hate is the way of the dark side.[65] You must break this cycle before it starts, before you have to explain to your pre-teen daughter that you love daddy, you're just not *in* love with him, and realize now you never really were, the realization of which came to you when you found out he had taken to banging his twenty-two-year-old secretary. If anyone's gonna be banging twenty-two-year-old secretaries, it should be you.

A lot of people believe that, when you talk about women getting what they want, being liberated and fulfilled and all that soft-serve mumbo jumbo, if sex is included even one iota in that dialogue then that that's what you're talking about. Casual sex. I don't know exactly how it happened, but in the last twenty years the word *fulfillment* became synonymous with having an orgasm. Not that I'm anti-orgasm. (That would make me crazy, wouldn't it? A crazy person. A crazy, frustrated person.) No, I'm just more pro-*you*. The whole you. The you that is a kick ass, go for what you want, have the time of your life every minute you can, strife slides off like water off a duck's back you.

65. Okay, I'm taking liberties with Yoda's quote now. But I gave him a call and he's cool with it. What a laid back dude.

And part of that should include having sex on your own terms, without commitment if you want it that way, without that sickening feeling you get in the morning after you sleep with a guy and realize you don't even really like the guy that much, would be happy to never see him again, except . . .

Except, you got attached. Shit. Now starts four months of gut-wrenching confusion, cajoling, wheedling, and generally emotionally noncommittal behavior on your part as you try to a) push him away out of disgust, and b) pull him toward you out of some vestigial genetically programmed mechanism that has imprinted him upon your psyche through the act of intercourse. When all along you could have been having a great time with your friends, eating pancakes or jetskiing or poking a beehive with a stick, not wasting one little bit of brain matter or corporeal electricity thinking about this knucklehead and why he told you he would call you and then seemed, somehow, to disappear, taking his phone line, apartment doorbell, and close circle of friends with him.

Sex is not love.

Chocolate is love. And puppies. And TiVo.

Get it straight.

McMarriage

There seems to be a strange bit of momentum toward getting women to give up some of the cooler things we've been able to do in recent years in favor of settling down. The zeitgeist seems to be all about getting you lovely young things married off and making babies as fast as humanly possible. According to reality television, we women are all just dying to get hitched, no matter how bizarre the context or how creepy the guy. (Evan Marriott? Yeesh!) There was even one show about how there were thousands of young, marriageable men in Alaska, furiously tapping maple trees and canning salmon and then going home to their chilly log cabins and darkened igloos, weeping into their mukluks because they were so alone. The show sent a group of *seemingly* mentally stable women up there to marry them off to the burly lumberjacks and salmon canners sight unseen, like a giant eight-pack of mail-order brides. There was a particularly disturbing shot of these women, in what looked like the last bunch of dresses to come off the deep-discount rack at David's Bridal, tramping through hip-deep snow, holding their trains high above their L.L. Bean duck boots, searching, searching for a man, *any* man, to put them out of their spinster misery. Where are we, nineteenth-century Russia? Have we forgotten about the high divorce rate, the epidemic of infidelity, the high price of marriage counseling?

Too many people are in a hurry to get married without understanding what marriage is about. Marriage isn't a carnival ride. *Step right up! Step right up! Toss the rings on the neck of the bottle and get yerself a prize! Three rings gets ya an unemployed slob with an El Camino and a backyard full of vicious pit bulls! Four gets ya a mohawked painter with a mommy complex and a chronic dope habit! Five gets ya a college graduate with impeccable dental hygiene and a raging foot fetish! Step right up! The choice is yours!*

You don't decide to get married and then find a husband. You meet and interact with a bunch of really interesting and intelligent men and then, if one suits your requirements, you consider hitching your wagon to theirs for all eternity. You *discover* a husband—you don't scrounge one up. Do it the first way, your marriage might last. Go with the latter and enjoy the lack of fulfillment and befuddling midlife crisis that is sure to come.

I'm going to go all out right now. Let me advance right

here, that the whole concept that women's sole goal in life is to snare a marriageable man is absolutely abhorrent. It implies that without some slob upon which to hang all your life's hopes and dreams, you are nothing. It is sexist and self-defeating, and *we are doing it to ourselves.*

Yes, yes, family and children are great, no doubt, but how can you be a good wife and mother when you're not a good person all by yourself? Hm?

Get with it! You're a hot young intelligent woman with interests, goals, and, most important, needs. And you are entitled to have those needs met to your complete satisfaction. Men have felt and understood this entitlement for years. In fact, they continue to feel this entitlement even after they've gotten married and had kids, which is why they spend their children's college funds on European convertibles and high-powered motorcycles shortly before leaving their wives for a well-endowed but mentally feeble secretary or catalog model or under-five actress with the medically augmented lips of a baboon.

Forget being sensitive and emotionally open and compassionate. That just gets you kicked in the teeth. We need to get back in touch with our raw, dirty, blood under the fingernails sense of entitlement: to be happy, to get what we want, to never, *ever* settle.

You may have surmised after reading thus far that I am antimarriage. I am not. I am actually quite happily married. Now, before you yell "fraud" at the top of your lungs, scaring your cat and angering the neighbors, who don't particularly like you anyway, hear me out. I believe in marriage. I believe deeply in the essence of it—the idea that you meet someone, fall in love, and realize you cannot live without them, in time bonding yourself to them for all eternity, promising to stand by them through the darkest and most difficult times in your lives, finally saying goodbye on your deathbeds. Romantic, huh?

Too bad plenty of Americans think that's bullshit. I think most people don't believe in marriage at all. "But," you protest, "of course they do! That's all anyone ever talks about! Every fiber of our cultural being sends the message that marriage solves all problems, from unplanned pregnancies to athlete's foot! All the political wonks wax bombastic about the sanctity of marriage, and how Congress is trying to destroy it with their Domestic Partners Act, along with the crazy kids and their MTV! There are books about how to get a guy to marry you, websites and magazine articles and Dr. Phil! Of course we believe in marriage!"

All these people who insist that marriage is heavenly, that it should be every American's sole goal to marry and have a family, that you should endeavor to trick, cajole, and maneuver that not-so-special guy into a commitment, are really anti-marriage, because they don't care if *your* marriage actually succeeds or fails. They just like promoting the *idea* of it. The idea of marriage is what's important to them, the concept, the ideal, the moral banner of it. It's a convenient moral position, a romantic stance to take. But to really maintain that true love, and the consecration of it through marriage, are important and worth defending, you have to admit that there are marriages that are not based on true love, or respect, or even basic human decency. To exalt good marriages, you have to accept that there are not so good ones, that bad ones exist, *and that those should be dissolved.* Let's face it, not everybody can be number one. Not every marriage, hell, probably not most of them, are entered into with any kind of understanding of what it takes to make a marriage last, of what kind of incredible, onerous, ongoing *job* sustaining a marriage can be. And that is because so many people are seduced by the *idea* of marriage these knuckleheads keep promoting. And it's a romantic idea, an idealized one, one that rests firmly on the fantasy of dresses and cakes and flowers, and not at all on the reality of overwhelming bills and divergent life goals and *why the hell can't he remember to keep his red T-shirts out of the white laundry* and *how many times do I have to tell her to put the toilet paper roll on so the flap hangs out and not in* and *who the hell peed on the floor in the bathroom?!?*[66]

If, instead of glamorizing marriage to the exclusion of everything else, these champions of matrimony presented it as a joy *and* a burden, a gift *and* a responsibility, people might be more careful about who they pulled the ol' trigger on, and thus better about not having to *unpull* the trigger. People get married all the time to people they know are

66. Face it. That could've been anybody.

wrong for them, to people who trigger their gag reflex *as they're walking down the aisle*, to people who they would counsel friends to dump unceremoniously and with a nice kick in the ass. And as they march down a flower-lined pathway to their doom, they cross their fingers, hoping against hope that marriage will change this person.

You cannot change people. Men know this. Why, why, why, with their limited understanding of the mechanics of human relationships, have they figured this out while we cannot? If people decide to change on their own, lucky you, you hit the lottery. But you cannot change them. And if you decide that being married is more important to you than being fulfilled, if you settle for the paunchy telemarketer who smells of sports ointment because you think you can't do any better, trust me, you won't. Marrying the wrong guy because you think your biological clock is running out is like trying to jam a square peg into a round hole. Or better yet, a noncommittal, emotionally remote, inarticulate and sexually lazy peg into a round hole.

Wanting a husband before you've learned how to live and love on your own terms is like trying to walk before you try to crawl; like trying to win a marathon without training for it. Sooner or later you're going to bonk, usually right into the open arms of a raging asshole. Marriage should be the thing you *arrive* at, a moment at which you look at each other and just know, that you're both ready to do whatever it takes to stay together. It's not a thing you plan out in your Palm Pilot. If you see it that way, I know a couple of good divorce lawyers.

If you see it the other way, congratulations. You're halfway there.

Go ahead. Get your swerve on.

〈 *SWERVE* 〉

Acknowledgments

I hesitate to thank anyone for their help in writing this book, as I am sure there are quite a few people who, now that it's completed, would rather have been left out of the whole thing. I'm sure most of them are composing a delicate way to call me a big fat liar as I write this. But far be it from me to be ungracious—they will just have to find some way to bear the heavy burden of my praise.

First of all, I have to profusely thank my manager and business partner William Ward, who encouraged me to write a book in the first place. (I can't remember if it was my idea or his, but that doesn't matter, now does it? *I'm* the one who had to write it.) He pushed me to do it, was an incredible sounding board, and had my back the whole way, peppering me with upbeat phone queries of "how's the book coming?" the entire time I was writing. At the time, it felt like burning-hot needles in my eyelids, but now I am very, *very* grateful. I'd also like to thank Mickey Barold, Bernie Cahill, and Jay Froberg. You all are my true posse.

I also want to deeply thank my publicist, Lisa Morbete, who encouraged me to stick to my guns and often pulled out her own heavy artillery when the situation called for it. She is my partner in crime and a constant inspiration. My agents, Brian Lipson and Dan Strone, who got into it when required and stayed out of it when appropriate. Thanks for being my silent wall of sound.

Big ups go to my editor, Amy Hughes, who championed my case from the start and worked tirelessly to make this happen. You stayed classy, enthusiastic, and engaged through it all. Lord knows I didn't make it easy for you. You got nads, girl. You got nads. Huge thanks also go to Brian Tart for taking the reins of this runaway cart and guiding it seamlessly into the barn. What does that mean, you ask? I don't quite know, but it sounds masterful, which he is.

I am blessed to have many brilliant, loving, and especially tolerant friends, from whom I draw constant inspiration, and also occasionally steal jokes. Two extraordinarily special people inspired fat chunks of this book: Todd Aument and Kimberly Lawrence Kol. I imagine you'd both rather have been left out of this focacta tome completely, but it's too late now, and so you must graciously accept my undying thanks and eternal admiration. You always bring the love. I also want to thank Nilos Glimidakis for, well, *being Nikos*. That's all that can be said about that.

To my family—my mom and my dad, for always pointing upwards and never down, for never questioning my ideas, for loving art and madness, and for leading by example. I wouldn't be half of who I am today if it wasn't for everything you are. You are an inspiration to me still. To my gorgeous grandmother for her constant love and patience. And to my sister, for being beautiful, smart, fierce, and absolutely, positively, no bullshit.

And finally, and *most* importantly, my husband Jeff, for laughing at my jokes, putting up with my mania, kissing me in my sleep, driving me to Fresno, and eating blueberry pancakes with me at four in the morning. You kick ass.

) **SWERVE** (

237

Aisha Tyler has a degree in government from Dartmouth College, which she blithely chucked for a career as an actress and stand-up comedian. She was the first female host of the Emmy Award–winning show *Talk Soup*, and has appeared in several films and television shows, including HBO's Emmy Award–winning *Curb Your Enthusiasm* and NBC's Emmy Award–winning *Friends*. As a writer she has contributed to *Jane, Glamour,* and *Vibe* magazines. She lives in Los Angeles. This is her first book, and man, is she excited about it.